A Troubled Faith

Faith

Do We Really Need God?

A Troubled Faith

Do We Really Need God?

ALAN REYNOLDS

A TROUBLED FAITH
by Alan Reynolds

Copyright © 2006 Alan Reynolds

alanreynolds@shaw.ca

ISBN # 1-894928-98-9

Published by Word Alive Press

WORD ALIVE

131 Cordite Road, Winnipeg, Manitoba, R3W 1S1
www.wordalive.ca

Printed in Canada

ACKNOWLEDGEMENTS

Thanks to Word Alive for choosing this manuscript from those submitted in their 2006 competition, and to the knowledgeable people there, especially Jeremy Braun and Caroline Schmidt, who provided much needed advice, and Evan Braun and Larissa Bartos, who have given help willingly.

The Word Guild directed me to Ray Wiseman, who provided very helpful editorial advice.

I want to thank several friends who read and responded to the manuscript with comments and criticisms: Elaine Foulkes, who got me going again when I had given up; Gordon Laird, who did the first read and whose keen eye noted many a slip; Dave Denholm in Alberta, Henry Tye in Prince Edward Island, and Dave Jones in North Carolina, who all provided helpful comments; my good friend, Arla Pinton, kept me going by providing constant support and encouragement; and most of all, Stew Clarke, my roommate from days at Pine Hill Divinity Hall, who did a thorough and careful reading and whose criticisms saved me from many an embarrassment.

I especially want to thank Brenda, my beautiful wife of forty-four years, who patiently endured the hours I spent in the study and with her keen eye for detail, gave the manuscript its final perusal and approval.

TABLE OF CONTENTS

Roots and Wings

Standing there, waiting for our friend, I had a very strange sensation. Something growing out of the bottom of my feet and reaching deep into the ground beneath me: roots, a sense of being deeply and organically connected to this place.

My wife Brenda and I were in London, England. We were standing in front of Wesley's Chapel, "the home church of world Methodism." My father had been ordained a minister of the Methodist Church in Canada in 1914, and though he later became part of the United Church of Canada, he remained a Methodist in heart and mind the rest of his life. Standing there, his spirit felt very close. My own roots in the Methodist tradition were still very much alive.

Wesley's Chapel is on City Road, just outside the boundaries of the old City of London. It was erected in 1778, after Methodism had become somewhat established, and named after the church's founder, John Wesley, whose life and ministry came to an end thirteen years later in 1791.

On the day we attended, the congregation, probably 150 people, was an interesting mix. Visitors from all over the world made up the majority of the group. A few elderly people represented the long-time members of the church, and there were a number of immigrants with solid Methodist roots in distant lands. The service was not dull, but also not especially inspiring. The preaching lacked both the passion and theology of John Wesley's preachings.

A day after our visit, when the thrill of visiting Wesley's Chapel had worn off, I began to reflect on the experience and on Methodism, its beginnings and subsequent development and history. As I did this, I began to feel a sadness about Methodism, the contrast between the early growth of Methodism, the roots from which it emerged and its current state and spirit, not unlike most of the traditional denominations of Christian faith.

In the beginning there was the man, John Wesley, completely dedicated to the Gospel. He is said to have travelled some 250,000 miles on horseback to preach the Gospel an estimated 40,000 to 50,000 times. His journal has been described as "the most amazing record of human exertion ever penned or endured." He once said, "The world is my parish!" And it was true. He took the Gospel outside the confines of the church walls, into the Godless world, the commons, and the fields where he gave it to the lay people. He preached to miners, emerging black-faced from the coal pits. His message was, "You are sons of God and heirs of salvation." He did not proclaim a message of condemnation and judgment. He gave them a sense of hope and pride, a sense of humanity. He held together the love of God and the love of neighbour. He organized aid to the poor and provided homes for orphans. His influence was instrumental in prison reform, the abolition of slavery, and many other humanitarian efforts. He gave the Gospel wings, and his followers, the Methodists, carried it to America and around the world.

Yet, such movements seem to lose their steam eventually. Movements become institutions, less inclined to risk, to change. Over the years, Methodism seems to have lost its wings. In fact, the Gospel would seem to have lost its wings. The worldview of the Middle Ages is no more. The courage of the Protestant Reformers seems lost. The confidence of the Evangelical era has been eroded by attacks from both science and philosophy. The optimism with which the twentieth century began has dissipated by the end of the century and left much of Christian faith in shock and even despair.

Christian faith, at the beginning of the twenty-first century, is a troubled faith, seemingly a faith in serious decline. Yet there are many who believe in the reality and truth of the life in Christ and who seek help in understanding and affirming their faith.

Acknowledging the decline of the power, influence, and confidence of the Christian church throughout the twenty-first century, this book seeks to establish a reasonable foundation for Christian faith. It will examine several key Christian beliefs that seem to be problems for those who own the name of Christ and for those seeking faith. I think of it as an *apologia*, a theological term meaning not an apology so much as a defense of the truth and relevancy of Christian faith in today's world. While I have always been a questioner, I do believe there is a reasonable foundation for Christian faith, and I believe in the importance of Christian faith in today's world and for our culture. I have had to struggle to understand my faith, so this is the result of a fair amount of spiritual and mental blood, sweat, and tears.

This book attempts to show that Christian faith is reasonable and can stand up to serious questioning.

THE CHAPEL[1]

A little aside from the main road,
becalmed in a last-century greyness,
there is the chapel, ugly, without the appeal
to the tourist to stop his car
and visit it. The traffic goes by,
and the river goes by, and quick shadows
of clouds, too, and the chapel settles
a little deeper into the grass.

But here once on an evening like this,
in the darkness that was about
his hearers, a preacher caught fire
and burned steadily before them
with a strange light, so that they saw
the splendour of the barren mountains
about them and sang their amens
fiercely, narrow but saved
in a way that men are not now.

_____

[1] R. S. Thomas, *Collect Poems 1945-1990*, Phoenix Press, a division of the Orion
Publishing Group Ltd., London, paperback edition published 2001, p 276.

CHAPTER 1

A TROUBLED FAITH

The Twentieth Century

In the past, it was understood that the mission of the church was to save others. At the present time, it seems the question is whether the church itself can be saved.

In the first decade of the twenty-first century, the Christian faith is a troubled faith, especially in those areas of the world traditionally regarded as Christian. Many of those who lived on the fringes have simply fallen away and given up any pretence of a life of faith. Others, who have never seriously questioned their faith, are considerably troubled to find that every belief, custom, and tradition is challenged. Those who seek to live by their faith, who face the changes and challenges of our time, find conflict and confusion instead of comfort and inspiration.

In contrast to how the twenty-first century seems to be shaping up, the twentieth century began with great optimism in the western world.

Herbert Spencer, who died in 1903, proclaimed, "Progress is not an accident, not a thing within human control, but a beneficent necessity ... due to the working of a universal law. So surely must the things we call evil and immorality disappear; so surely must man become perfect." The long, prosperous, and relatively peaceful reign of Queen Victoria had lent its name to an era, and not only the British had spread their versions of civilization across the face of the earth, but other European imperialisms as well.

Technology was producing wonderful things that promised a better and brighter life. Thomas Edison had produced the first phonograph in 1877 and the first workable electric light bulb in 1879. The American Centennial Exposition, held in Philadelphia in

1876, exhibited one of the first telephones. In 1904, Otis Bros. patented an "electronic lifting device" that made practical the construction of buildings more than four or five stories high. A few "horseless carriages" were making their initial appearance, and on December 17, 1903, Orville and Wilbur Wright achieved the first successful sustained and controlled flight through the air. "Glory to Man in the highest! For Man is the master of things," sang the poet Swinburne in his "Hymn of Man."

The Christian church, though divided (not only between Eastern Orthodox and Roman Catholic, but also between Catholic and Protestant—and Protestant into a thousand pieces), was influential and wealthy. A prime minister or president would tread carefully in matters that concerned Christian sensibilities. On Sunday mornings, people filled churches of all traditions (and most Protestant churches in the evenings as well). Christian missionaries spread the Gospel to all parts of the world. Hopefulness was easy and progress was everywhere.

In 1913, Walter Rauschenbusch, prophet of the Social Gospel, declared, "The larger part of the task of Christianizing the social order is already accomplished," and John R. Mott, student secretary of the International Committee of the YMCA (Young Men's Christian Association) and Chair of the Student Volunteer Movement, adopted the slogan, "The world for Christ in this generation."[2] Christian congregations sang with conviction,

> The day of dawning brotherhood
> Breaks on our eager eyes,
> And human hatreds flee before
> The radiant Eastern skies.[3]

Then came the two most destructive wars in human history, an economic depression of deep consequence, and the Holocaust (surely one of the most significant events of the twentieth century for Jews and Christians alike). Atomic warfare and other immense forms of destruction also arrived on the scene. Today, we have

---

[2] Mott was awarded the Nobel Prize for peace in 1946 for his work in church and missionary movements.

[3] This and the quotations from Herbert Spencer and Walter Rauschenbusch are from Harry Emerson Fosdick, *A Faith for Tough Times*, Harper and Brothers, Publishers, New York, 1952, pp. 28-30.

become accustomed to living in a world that has unknown quantities of weapons of mass destruction. We live with the knowledge that humanity has the power to destroy itself, and not only itself but also the earth on which it depends for its own existence. Kenneth Boulding wrote,

> We may dramatize the present world situation by saying that every day the hand of fate dips into a bag containing one black ball amid many white balls: the ball of nuclear disaster. Up to now, every day, fate has brought up a white ball, and the world goes on, but the black ball is still in the bag, and as long as it remains there no one can feel very secure about his future.[4]

Our world is perilously and increasingly divided by rich and poor, and with economic problems that defy the imagination. We live in a world with increasing evidence that our whole ecological system is breaking down. Ever-accelerating change causes extreme stress in our common life, resulting in anger, frustration, depression, and disenchantment. All these have led, in turn, to the increased use of drugs, legal and illegal, the breakdown of marriage and family, the collapse of traditional religious belief and moral values, and the worsening of all-too-prevalent mental illnesses. Ancient enmities have erupted in bloody and mutually destructive conflicts, notably in the Near East and Ireland. Intertribal warfare in various parts of Africa sometimes amounts to genocide, as in Rwanda.

As the twentieth century ended, hopelessness and prevalent despair replaced the general spirit of hopefulness and civil optimism of the beginning of the century. The Y2K panic, and the fear of economic and social collapse, spoke volumes of the insecurity and anxiety of the time.

Attacks on Faith

Nineteenth century thinkers had earlier attacked the underpinnings of the Christian faith, raising questions about the truth of the Bible

---

[4] Kenneth Boulding, *The Meaning of the Twentieth Century: the Great Transition*, (Vol. 34 of the World Perspective Series, planned and edited by Ruth Nanda Anshen), New York: Harper & Row, 1964, p. 91.

and the reality of the spiritual realm. Karl Marx advanced his understanding of historical materialism. Charles Darwin presented vast evidence to support his theory that life had evolved naturally and over a much longer period than the Bible recorded. Sigmund Freud analyzed the human psyche. To the popular mind, it seemed that Marx removed God from human history, Darwin from nature, and Freud from the soul.

Positivism, the philosophy of Auguste Comte, restricted knowledge to mathematics and scientific knowledge derived from phenomena observed by the senses. Comte prophesied that Notre Dame Cathedral would be a temple of Positivism within one hundred years. Pierre-Simon Laplace said of the existence of God, "I have no need of that hypothesis." The poets of the nineteenth century, notably Tennyson and Browning, agonized over their doubts. Christians could no longer have the intellectual assurance they had once professed and, as the force of such philosophical attacks on the faith were increasingly felt on the popular level, more and more common people, members of the various Christian traditions, became increasingly, if unconsciously, insecure in their faith.

There was a whole worldview behind these attacks on Christian faith, a worldview that had gained common acceptance. It was developed from the thought and work of great philosophers and scientists at the beginnings of the modern era—Bacon, Galileo, Newton, and Descartes. So firmly has this worldview found acceptance in the modern era that its presuppositions and assumptions have only been seriously questioned in recent years. In the closing decades of the twentieth century, it seemed that a process of realization occurred, an awareness of the limitations of scientific inquiry and recognition of the validity of other kinds of knowledge.

Decline in Numbers and Influence

Since 1900, the population of the United States has grown by 300% while there are only 50% more churches. There were 27 churches for every 10,000 people in 1900, but today that number is down to 11.[5] In 1960, total mainline church membership topped at just over 29 million. By 2000, this number had fallen to 22 million. This represents a 21% drop in mainline membership.[6]

The United Methodist Church, the largest Protestant denomination in the United States, claimed 6.1% of the population in 1900, but only 3.6% in 1990. It peaked in 1970, and since then has lost approximately 18% of its lay membership. The Methodist Church in Great Britain claimed 770,406 members in 1900, and just 424,540 in 1990.[7] The triennial figures for 1996 stated that Methodism there was "in terminal decline."[8]

The so-called "mainline denominations" have been largely sidelined. They were once regarded as the backbone of our civil society and enjoyed a kind of *de facto* establishment status. They have been largely disestablished.[9] Some evangelical churches are thriving, but to this point at least, they have not represented a significant percentage of the population. The confidence of most church traditions is not strong, and the depth of conviction of individual believers has been shown to be generally shallow. Historian Mark Noll wrote a critique of Evangelicalism in 1994 titled *The Scandal of the Evangelical Mind,* and generally reaffirmed his criticisms ten years later.[10] In Canada, way back in 1965, Canadian novelist and historian Pierre Burton wrote *The Comfortable Pew*, a critique of the Canadian Anglican Church of the time.[11] Subsequently, sociologist Reginald Bibby, in *Fragmented Gods* and subsequent books, has indicated the fragmentation of

---

[5] Ed Stitzer, *Planting New Churches in a Post Modern Age,* Nashville: Broadman & Holman Publishers, 2003.

[6] *Christianity Today*, August, 2003, p. 37.

[7] David Hempton, *Methodism: Empire of the Spirit*, Yale University Press, New Haven and London, 2005, pp. 212 & 214.

[8] "Church Decline: showing what matters most? Peter Edwards in the Epworth Review, Vol. 29.2, April, 2002, p. 54.

[9] "Establishment" meant that the national church was secured and supported by the state, as the Church of England in England or the Lutheran Church in Germany.

[10] "Ten years after the publication of *The Scandal of the Evangelical Mind,* I remain largely unrepentant." (*First Things*, October 2004, pp. 34-39).

[11] Pierre Berton, *The Comfortable Pew, McClelland and Stewart , Toronto, 1965.*

Canadian religion and the tendency to "Religion à la carte" and "Religion as a consumer item."[12]

Divisions, not only between Protestant and Catholic, but between liberal and conservative (modernist and fundamentalist, ecumenical and evangelical), have blurred the meaning and blunted the effectiveness of the Gospel. This is especially true of the unfortunate and unnecessary dispute between evolution and Creationism, which keeps rearing its head despite being irrelevant to the Biblical stories of creation.[13]

The higher courts or bureaucratic structures of mainline denominations have taken stands that are out of tune with their general membership, and have not been able to explain their position to their members or convince them of their rightness. To make matters worse, such positions have been taken as the result of superficial analysis or ideological convictions. American socio-logist Peter Berger, himself a churchman and a liberal, wrote,

> When I go to church or read church publications I'm irritated when I'm confronted with statements that I consider to be empirically flawed ... The irritation deepens when these terrible simplifications are proclaimed to me in tones of utter certitude and moral urgency.[14]

Then there were the scandals, crossing a broad denominational spectrum, from Roman Catholic to Pentecostal. Many clergy, members of a profession traditionally respected and often revered, showed themselves to have feet of clay and evidently many could not keep their minds above their belts.

Television evangelists Jimmy Bakker (exposed for income tax fraud) and Jimmy Swaggert (for consorting with prostitutes) lost their popular followings. At the other end of the denominational spectrum, dozens of Roman Catholic priests, required to practise celibacy, were found to be paedophiles, often taking advantage of

---

[12] Reginald Bibby, *Fragmented Gods: the Poverty and Potential of Religion in Canada*, Irsin Publishing, Toronto, 1987. The references are to chps. 4 & 8.

[13] See Alan Reynolds, *Reading the Bible for the Love of God*, Brazos Press, Grand Rapids, MI, 2003, pp. 62-64.

[14] Peter Berger, "Different Gospels: The Social Sources of Apostasy," in *American Apostasy: The Triumph of Other Gospels*, Grand Rapids, Michigan: W. B. Eerdmans, 1989, pp. 8-9.

altar boys. Worse, in some areas it was shown that the hierarchy of the church had tried to cover up the situation.

Overseas, with the breakdown of colonialism, many nationals who had espoused Christianity began to turn back to their national traditions and beliefs. Church historian Kenneth Scott Latourette, in his *History of Christianity,* had called the nineteenth century "The Great Century" because of its missionary expansion.[15] One wonders what he would have called the twentieth century.

Many ordinary church members, bruised and bewildered by these onslaughts to their faith, either quietly stopped attending or, if they remained faithful, continued dispirited and in low morale. In the early years of the twenty-first century, those who own the name "Christian" are suffering a loss of nerve. Gone is the religious confidence of the nineteenth and early twentieth centuries. Faced with the commitment of Muslim extremist suicide bombers,[16] willing to give their life for their faith, the disciples of Jesus Christ seem strangely silent and withdrawn. North American Christians cling to their comforts, snuggling down in their comfortable pews. But their sleep is a troubled sleep.

Things Which Cannot Be Shaken

Our modern western culture was assumed to have been Christian because the Christian church was such an important part of the political establishment and a powerful influence on the life, politics, morals, and ethos of the culture. But it has become increasingly apparent that the scientific worldview has become pervasive, and many of the assumptions of the modern era are based on our contemporary scientific views, which are antithetical

---

[15] Kenneth Scott Latourette, *A History of Christianity*, "The Great Century: Growing Repudiation Paralleled by Abounding Vitality and Unprecedented Expansion, AD1815 – AD1914," Harper and Brothers, Publishers, New York, 1953, pp. 1063-1349.

[16] In Islam, it is indeed very difficult to separate religion and politics. Blowing yourself up is not only a type of terrorism, it is an expression of (national or international) social protest. Most suicide bombers evidently are empowered to do what they do not only by their desire for social change for their people and with the support of fellow believers, but also in their own confidence in the promises of reward in a world to come in the Qu'ran.

to Christian faith. The debate between science and religion, which in the mind of most goes back to Galileo, is taking on new dimensions much deeper than the fuss raised currently by the Creationist movement.

> Empiricism insists that all knowledge is based on observation, experimentation, and verification and leads to belief in a self-sufficient universe that can be understood and explained on its own terms, without the need for any reference to the transcendent or to God…
>
> Belief in natural causation, the law of cause and effect, leads to determinism, which in turn leads to an understanding of reality as mechanical, including the ways in which we view the origin of life and the nature of our humanity.
>
> Emphasis on analysis (observation and experimentation) leads to increased specialization (reductionism), which results in the loss of a sense of purpose and any place for value. You can take a machine apart to see how it works, but you have to put it back together to understand its purpose and put it to use. Specialization has resulted in many wonderful discoveries, but it cannot unite discrete parts into a meaningful whole.[17]

Lesslie Newbigin, first Bishop of the Church of South India and a missionary in India for some forty years, retired and returned to England late in the twentieth century. He began to ask why the Christian churches, strong and vital in much of the world, were weak and in decline in so-called Christian countries. The British Council of Churches asked Newbigin to write a small book dealing with the cause of such decline. Titled *The Other Side of 1984*, it raised much discussion of the relation of the churches to modern western culture. He asked, "What would be involved in a missionary encounter between the gospel and this whole way of perceiving, thinking, and living that we call 'modern western culture?'"[18]

This led to the Warfield Lectures given at Princeton University in March, 1984, published as *Foolishness to the Greeks*, an examination of those presuppositions of modern culture showing

---

[17] Reynolds, *Reading the Bible,* pp. 26-27.
[18] Lesslie Newbigin, *Foolishness to the Greeks: the Gospel and Western Culture*, William B. Eerdmans Publishing Company, Grand Rapids, Michigan, 1986, p.1.

them to be adversative to Christian faith. Newbigin hit a chord to which many in the church responded as they sought a deeper understanding of the ennui of our present culture and the reason for the church's decline.[19]

I was ordained a minister of the United Church of Canada in 1954, post World War II, a time of renewed hopefulness. Nazism had been defeated. The newly formed United Nations promised peace. Veterans returned to civilian life, jobs, and families. Many took advantage of government educational programs. Proposed social reforms, such as the Beveridge Report in England, promised a society that cared for the welfare of all its people. Churches again were filled with young families dressed in their Sunday best.

The ideals of the 1950's would not last, and neither would the church attendance or the self-satisfaction. Now, at the other end of my ministry, I wonder about the future of the church and of the faith that I still cherish and still believe.

Ours is a troubled faith, disturbed, confused, and disordered. But it is not an empty faith.

The letter of the New Testament we call "Hebrews" was written in a time much like our own and for just such a community of faith, also troubled and confused. This letter, probably written at the time of the destruction of Jerusalem and the temple by the armies of Rome in 70AD, is very conscious of the transience of life. It was written in a time of great turmoil, upheaval, and great destruction. The "holy city" (Jerusalem) and the "holy temple" represented to the Jewish people (and to the Jewish Christians as well) all that was constant and abiding, that which God would never allow destroyed.

But now both city and temple had been totally destroyed, and an unknown disciple of Jesus writes to point out to these Jewish Christians, in the midst of all this uncertainty and mutability, that there are "things which cannot be shaken."

---

[19] The reasons for the decline of the Christian church through the 20th century are many. For a theological analysis, I can do no better than refer you to Newbigin's later works. In addition to *Foolishness to the Greeks,* note T*he Gospel In A Pluralist Society*, (William B. Eerdmans Publishing Company, Grand Rapid, MI, and WCC Publications, Geneva, 1989), and *Truth to Tell: The Gospel As Public Truth*, (William B. Eerdmans Publishing Company, Grand Rapids, MI, and WCC Publications, Geneva, 1991).

The object of your faith, he tells them, is not an earthly mountain like Mount Sinai, where God gave the people the Ten Commandments, a mountain which can be touched, which shook and quaked and burned and smoked at the presence of God. No, the object of your faith, and of ours, is the heavenly Jerusalem, Mount Zion rather than Mount Sinai, "the city of the living God," "not made with hands," the Kingdom which is unshakeable, founded upon the covenant of God in the blood of Jesus Christ our Lord.

> *You stand before Mount Zion and the city of the living God, heavenly Jerusalem, before myriads of angels in joyful assembly, and those whose names are written in heaven, and God the Judge of all.* (Hebrews 12:22-24)

In fact, says the writer, those false things in which you have put your trust, the things of the earth and the created order, are being shaken and destroyed precisely so that the things which cannot be shaken may be distinguished and revealed.

A changing and chaotic day such as ours shows the impermanence of most things, but will also reveal, to those who seek them, the things that don't change, that which is lasting and permanent. It shows us what is true and what is false, what is good and what is truly evil. It can, if we will let it, correct our way of living and purify our faith.

Sometimes even the mountains seem shaken, and the things which we considered most durable, most abiding, perhaps considered the very basis of our faith and life, are ripped and torn apart. But through all the turmoil and the change, that which is finally true and abiding can be revealed to us.

For Those of Troubled Faith

Christian faith, at the beginning of the twenty-first century, is a troubled faith, seemingly a faith in serious decline. Yet many believe in the reality and truth of the life in Christ and seek help in understanding and affirming their faith.

This book is an *apologia*, a theological term. An "apology," in this sense, is not so much an expression of regret for wrongs committed as it is a defence and explication of the truth of Christian faith for the present time. In a day that says, "I feel," rather than "I think," it attempts to show that Christian faith is reasonable. In spite of its present depressed spirit, Christian faith can stand up to serious questioning. In a day of renewed super-stitions, it tries to show that Christian faith does make sense.

Christians have lived in positions of assumed privilege in western culture for many, many years. Suddenly we find ourselves on the defensive, challenged and lacking in confidence, unable to find the right words or the right actions in the world today. I write now with the prayer and the hope that these words may help those who own the name of Jesus Christ to find their voice again.

This book is for those of troubled faith, those who have difficulty finding answers to their many questions, and maybe even those who acknowledge no faith.

It is also for those who were brought up by parents of nominal faith. They believed in God and sent you to Sunday School, perhaps attended church regularly themselves and taught you a little prayer to say at bedtime. But their faith lacked any real depth and fervour.

When you went to university, there didn't seem much place for God in higher education. Often professors would question Christian belief or make fun of those Bible stories you learned in Sunday School, raising questions you had never been prepared to consider or answer.

There seemed to be no need for God in the rest of life either. Friends didn't go to church. Instead they enjoyed tennis, football, hockey, parties, picnics at the beach, weekends at the lake, hiking, and skiing. God wasn't part of it, and yet life went happily along.

There were, of course, questions. Big questions. Sometimes you had long discussions with close friends. What does it all mean? How will it end? Is our life just a few moments out of the eons of time and that's it? Is it all meaningless, a kind of illusion?

And yet there is so much that is wonderful, so much meaning, so much joy. There seems to be something there, some sense of meaning, or purpose. You think. You wonder. Do we really need God?

CHAPTER 2

DO WE REALLY NEED GOD?

*"Thou hast made us for Thyself,
and our hearts are restless
till they find their rest in Thee."*[20]

The Disappearing Deity

Recently, Brenda and I once stayed several days at a B&B. It was a lovely spot and our hosts were very nice people, honest and good-hearted. Both were very intelligent, knowledgeable and gracious. They have a fine home, worth close to a million dollars. They have a beautiful yard and garden, elegant furnishings, two cars, and every gadget and toy available for modern living, from computers to coffee makers, from the latest in automated heating to the finest in cookware.

They enjoy their life, their home, their family and friends. They like to travel, and do. Like so many of our modern western culture, they are evidently quite self-sufficient. They live life to the fullest. When death comes to one of them, it will bring grief, but like millions of people down through the ages of human history, they will accept the inevitable and carry on as bravely as they can.

Our host and hostess are typical of the millions of people who comprise our post-Christian western culture. They are comfortable and reasonably happy. Do they have any need of God?

---

[20] From the opening paragraph of Augustine's *Confessions,* and in my opinion among the truest words ever spoken or written. *The Confessions of St. Augustine*, trans. F. J. Sheed, Sheed and Ward, London, 1945, p. 1.

On the North American continent, public prayer and Bible reading used to be required in the school system. Now they are not allowed in public schools and God is not mentioned in most of our educational systems. God is doing a disappearing act in most public functions, excepting in times of death or disaster. The "Prayer of Invocation," invoking or calling on the presence of God, is less and less common at meetings of city councils or at university graduation ceremonies.

Though undeniable pockets of poverty exist in our culture, we are relatively prosperous in comparison to most of the world and most of human history. We have wonderful hospitals and medical treatment. We have great universities and most of us are well-educated. Things were never so good. As a culture, we seem to be doing quite well without God, thank you.

It may be that we are what has been called "a cut-flower culture," severed from our roots in the Biblical tradition and flourishing only on the spiritual capital accumulated by our forebears. But we are flourishing, at least in a general sense, in spite of the fact that we have largely dropped God out of our common life. It may be that people have come to realize that no-god is better than bad religion. And let's face it; down through the history of the human race, most religion has been bad religion.

Do we really need God?

I am a minister of the Gospel, having spent much of my time and effort seeking to help people find faith in God. You would naturally expect me to answer, "Yes, we really do need God."

However, in recent years since retirement, I've had freedom to re-examine my own beliefs, to ask myself frankly whether people and any human culture does, in fact, have any need of God. I now don't have to go to church. I don't have to believe. I have watched as many of my friends drifted away from any seeming need of God, even some in my own family. In a general sense, my whole culture seems to be drifting away from any sense of God's presence in daily life.

I find most people are kind. In the past year, I've had a lot of experience with our health care system—hospital stays, day surgeries, tests and X-rays, and visits to various doctors. Without exception, I have been met with kindness and care, without any reference to God or religion. I ask myself, do we really need God?

Then I read today's newspaper. What a catalogue of grief and sin! Not only natural suffering and death, in which most people still turn to God, but a documentary of our inhumanity: murder (ghastly chain-saw murder), rape, drunkenness, and the irresponsibility of prominent people. Perhaps most terrible of all is the abuse of children, terrible physical and sexual abuse. There is controversy, currently over same-sex marriage. And there is triviality, whole sections of the paper dedicated to food and clothing, cars and sports, and items such as one piece announcing Madonna's new perfume.

All this in today's newspaper. Are we crazy? Insane? Both?

It seems so obvious, so very clear—we really do need God, and if we can't find God, we will make for ourselves other gods, or at least some form of religion. But I make my claim in the face of a culture that responds with a resounding "No."

Secular Humanism and Enduring Religion

Julian Huxley (1887-1985) was a member of a famous family. He was a brother of novelist Aldous Huxley and Nobel Laureate Andrew Fielding Huxley. His grandfather was Thomas Huxley, who coined the word "agnostic" to describe his own belief that God could not be known. Julian promoted what he called "evolutionary humanism." He championed a non-theistic "religion without revelation" and wrote that "Man's destiny is to be the sole agent for the future evolution of this planet, and he must face it unaided by outside help." After a succession of highly visible administrative posts, Huxley became the founding Director-General of UNESCO (the United Nations Educational, Scientific and Cultural Organization). He used these positions to advocate his gospel of human progress dependent not upon God or any spiritual or supernatural agency, but upon humanity alone.[21]

Secular humanism, the belief that humanity must do without God which Huxley called evolutionary humanism, has become the

---

[21] Note Edward J. Larson, *Evolution: The Remarkable History of a Scientific Theory*, The Modern Library, New York, 2004, pp. 248-9. Note Julian Huxley, *UNESCO: Its Purpose and Its Philosophy*, Public Affairs Press, Washington, 1947.

religion of many of the intelligentsia of modern western culture, even in many respects the unofficial official religion of the culture itself.[22]

Yet over it all, there hangs a slight sense of suspense, as though judgment is about to fall upon us. It's like the child who said, "I haven't said my prayers for five nights now, and nothing's happened yet." Always, there's the "yet."

We may seem to do well without God, but something is certainly wrong, and humanity appears to be inevitably and incurably religious. "There is something eternal in religion which is destined to survive all the particular symbols in which religious thought has successively enveloped itself," wrote Emil Durkheim.[23]

The vast majority of people still "believe in God" and indications are that most people pray,[24] especially when faced by insecurity, danger, disease, or death. Some people would call themselves spiritual rather than religious, perhaps in an effort to disassociate themselves from what they consider bad religion. Others, who do not have a formal religion, develop social practices and rituals that take on the social semblance of religion.

The word "culture" comes from a root meaning *to inhabit*, with the intimation that human habitation implies cultivation, bringing order out of chaos, turning the wilderness into a garden. Closely associated with the word "culture," etymologically and historically, is the word "cult," implying that religion is an essential piece of the art of cultivation. The word "culture" may seem at present to have lost its religious intimation, yet in every culture, from earliest days of human history, religion has seemed to be a part of human life.

---

[22] Secular humanism is, however, not the inevitable result of modernity, but rather the result of a restricted understanding of human knowledge and how it is obtained. It would claim that our knowledge, the understanding of our human experience, is restricted to mathematics or objective verification (or "falsification"), or to pure or practical reason. I would affirm that our knowledge includes that which is not quantifiable, values that are not necessarily subject to reason, an understanding of the personal.

[23] Emil Durkheim, *Elementary Forms of Religious Life*, Unwin, London, 1915, p. 427.

[24] For example, Time (Canada) reported in 2003 that 81% of Canadians claim to believe in God, 66% strongly, and seven out of ten consider prayer important. (*Time*, November 24, 2003, Vol. 162, No. 21, Time Canada Ltd., Toronto, pp. 72ff.)

Even today, in this most secular age, the most secular situations take on the semblance of religious, though not Christian, observances. Shopping malls are like great temples, and professional sporting events have their set rituals. Entertainment is the popular religion of our time. Its devotees sit in rapt attention in front of the television set or the computer screen, or make great pilgrimages to Las Vegas or Disney World. As Undershaft says, in Shaw's play, *Major* Barbara, "I am a Millionaire. That is my religion."[25]

We all tend, in some way, to something outside ourselves, something beyond. We adopt, consciously or unconsciously, social practices, personal habits and attitudes, which may broadly be called religious. While there are some people who seem to get by with no obvious expression of religion, it seems that we all have to some degree a built-in awareness of the ultimate. It is hard to imagine any human being completely lacking in what Paul Tillich called "ultimate concern," by which I mean in this context a concern with the ultimate. "Being religious is being unconditionally concerned, whether this concern expresses itself in secular or (in the narrower sense) religious forms."[26]

Humanity, it seems, is incurably religious.

Life After God

Douglas Coupland, originator of the term Generation X, has thought about human life without God, and has expressed his concern powerfully and poetically. He writes with real insight of a generation generously gifted in material things but spiritually deprived. For me, his most impressive and expressive book is *Life*

---

[25] George Bernard Shaw, *Major Barbara,* Act 2, in *A Prose Anthology*, edit. Hm M Burton, Longman Group Ltd., London, 1958, p. 78

[26] Paul Tillich, *The Protestant Era*, trans. James Luther Adams, Phoenix Books, The University of Chicago Press, Abridged Edition, 1957, p. xii. Tillich spoke of both unconditional and ultimate concern. "Our ultimate concern is that which determines our being or non-being." (*Systematic Theology*, Vol. 1, Nisbet & Co. Ltd., London, 1953, p. 17.) Tillich is here speaking more specifically of theology rather than religion.

After God,[27] "a collection of short stories told by thirty-something narrators who are still bruised from their painful twenties and are now dealing with the hardships of divorce, depression and spiritual confusion—trying to make sense of what it means to have been raised by the first generation of parents that stopped believing in God."[28] Coupland's novels are intensely personal and obviously autobiographical.[29] He writes about Vancouver, notably North Vancouver and West Vancouver, the advantaged social locations where he grew up. He writes about his teenaged years, "a life of earthly salvation on the edge of heaven." [30]

> As suburban children we floated at night in swimming pools the temperature of blood: pools the color of Earth as seen from outer space. We would skinny-dip... Our minds would be blank and our eyes closed as we floated in warm waters, the distinction between our bodies and our brains reduced to nothing.... Ours was a life lived in paradise and thus it rendered any discussion of transcendental ideas pointless.[31]

But all that changed over the years. He chronicles the subsequent lives of his friends, empty of meaning, empty even of feeling. The narrator, "Scout," reflects,

> I think the price we paid for our golden life was an inability to fully believe in love; instead we gained an irony that scorched everything it touched. And I wonder if this irony is the price we paid for the loss of God.[32]

He describes himself as "a broken person."

---

[27] Douglas Coupland, *Life After God,*, POCKET BOOKS, a division of Simon & Schuster Inc. New York, 1994. Note "1,000 Years (Life After God)," pp. 269 ff.

[28] Christopher Yates, "Hope for the Denarrated Self: Revisiting a Decade of Douglas Coupland," *CRUX: A Quarterly Journal o f Christian Thought and Opinion published by Regent College,* Regent College, Vancouver, Canada, March, 2003, Vol. XXXIX, No. 1, p. 4. Coupland's later writings are perhaps more pessimistic and seem to imply that he has never found the God he needs.

[29] "I write about my own life always. It has never been otherwise." Quoted by Matthew Gilbert, *The Boston Globe,* 16 March, 1994, quoted by Yates, op. cit., p. 3.

[30] *Life After God*, p. 273.

[31] *Life After God, pp. 271-273.*

[32] *Life After God*, p. 273.

> I have an unsecure and vaguely crappy job with an amoral corporation so that I don't have to worry about money. I put up with halfway relationships so as not to have to worry about loneliness. I have lost the ability to recapture the purer feelings of my younger years in exchange for a streamlined narrow-mindedness that I assumed would propel me to "the top." What a joke![33]

He finds himself on a wasted, clear-cut mountainside on the west coast of Vancouver Island, in an old tent, "in the dark and the rain … knowing that this is the end of some aspect of my life, but also a beginning—the beginning of some unknown secret that will reveal itself to me soon. All I need do is ask and pray."[34] There, standing in the chill of a mountain stream, he says,

> Now—here is my secret:

> I tell it to you with an openness of heart that I doubt I shall ever achieve again, so I pray that you are in a quiet room as you hear these words. My secret is that I need God—that I am sick and can no longer make it alone. I need God to help me give, because I no longer seem to be capable of giving; to help me be kind, as I no longer seem capable of kindness; to help me love, as I seem beyond being able to love.[35]

Coupland points to a cold, cynical, loveless future without God. And there are many indications that what lies ahead of us is a life rich in appearance but empty in content, mechanically efficient but lacking any personal warmth. It is the future forecast by so many of our poets, artists, musicians, and filmmakers, from T. S. Eliot to Steven Spielberg, Aldous Huxley among them. It is a future that impinges on our present, and in the midst of our comforts and prosperity it is a future that we know for sure we do not want.

---

[33] *Life After God,* p. 309.
[34] *Life After God,* pp. 316 & 352.
[35] *Life After God,* p. 359.

Our Need of God

I believe we really do need God and that need is evidenced by our inevitable religiosity. As the Bible tells us, we are "created in the image of God" (Genesis 1:27), which means, I take it, not that God looks like us or that we are in some way divine, but that we are created for relationship with God and without that, there is a God-shaped hole in our hearts. As Augustine said in his *Confessions* (noted at the beginning of this chapter), "Thou hast made us for Thyself, and our hearts are restless till they find their rest in Thee."

Religion is our reaching out to find God, and if we reject the God or gods we are given, we will create our own. Humanity, as I say, seems to be incurably religious.

At this point, I do not argue for any particular understanding of God, nor advocate any special religion, but simply affirm that we will worship something, whether the gods of entertainment or consumerism, or the seeking of salvation through science and technology.

We may go from day to day living on a superficial level, a one-dimensional existence, finding a passing pleasure in our occupations with toys, whether cars or fishing gear, art or sex objects. We may find a certain and very real fulfillment in our personal relationships—family and friends. These all form the horizontal dimension of our existence.

But there is also a vertical dimension. There are those times, sometimes little more than moments, when the depths of our being open up and we sense that we are created for eternity. Marcus Borg calls them "thin places," a phrase from Celtic Christianity.[36] Poet Francis Thompson points to the same unseen dimension of our human existence:

> I dimly guess what Time in mists confounds;
> Yet ever and anon a trumpet sounds
> From the hid battlements of Eternity;
> Those shaken mists a space unsettle, then
> Round the half-glimpsed turrets

---

[36] Marcus Borg, *The Heart of Christianity: Rediscovering a Life of Faith*, HarperSanFrancisco, 1st edition, pp. 155f.

Slowly wash again.
But not ere him who summoneth
I first have seen.[37]

Consider some of the obvious ways we need God.

We call upon God in times of personal need—whether cold and hungry and lost in the northern woods or simply as an act of desperation when we face an exam for which we haven't prepared. There are of course the bad times when we, or those we love deeply, are terminally ill, or when we are going through some other serious personal crisis.

We cry to God in times of mortal peril. "There are no atheists in the foxholes," declared Father Cummings in a field sermon on Bataan in 1942,[38] and eighteenth century English poet, Edward Young, wrote "By night an atheist half believes in God.[39]

We call upon God in times of national disaster. As a result of the terrorist attack on September 11, 2001, when America was hurting, it seemed that the whole nation was suddenly religious, calling upon God again and again at national gatherings and civic events across the country. "God bless America" temporarily replaced "The Star Spangled Banner" as the national anthem, in popular custom if not by act of Congress.

We often turn to God when we feel guilty. Isn't this the reason guilt is a problem for psychiatry, because we cannot forgive ourselves? Guilt is as much a religious problem as a psychological one.

For instance, there is a poignant scene in the film *Schindler's List*. The commandant of the Plaszow work camp, Amon Goeth, a cruel man, shoots Jewish prisoners on a whim. Schindler convinces him that the power lies not in shooting people but in pardoning them, as an emperor might pardon a thief. When Lisiek, his stable boy, leaves his expensive saddle on the ground, Goeth excuses him. Again, when the boy is unable to remove stains from

---

[37] FrancisThompson, *The Hound of Heaven*, The Peter Pauper Press, Mount Vernon, New York, p. 22.
[38] William Thomas Cummings, from Carlos P. Romulo, *I Saw The Fall Of The Philippines (1942).*
[39] *Night* V, l. 177.

the bathtub, the commandant, with an evident growing sense of power, tells him, "I pardon you," and gives the three-finger sign of the Trinity. Later, while shaving, he looks at himself in the mirror, makes the sign of the Trinity, and says to himself, "I pardon you." After a moment of thought, he takes his rifle and, for no apparent reason, kills the young Jewish lad. Why? Because he has realized that he cannot forgive himself for the terrible things he has done. Only God can do that.

As with guilt, so with gratitude—it seems there are times when there is nowhere to turn but to God. There are those moments of transcendent beauty or joy, "a sunset touch, a fancy from a flower-bell, someone's death, a chorus ending from Euripides,"[40] when our hearts scream to say, "Thank you!" Even when we seem to have no need of God, we still have a need to say "thank you." And it's always, remember, some*one*! It's never some*thing*! We don't say, "thank it"—we say "thank *you*!" We don't thank the cow for milk, or the tree for fruit. We may be grateful when rain falls from the sky, or for a beautiful fall day, or for flowers in the garden, but we don't thank the sky, the sun, or the plant. We may be grateful for some escape from injury or death, but we don't give thanks to a very fickle Lady Luck. We don't say, "thank it," we say "thank you!" It's a response instead of a reaction, implying a personal relationship.

It seems that our sense of gratitude must reach behind the stage of our human existence to the One we call God. When the feeling of gratitude for the beauty and the joy of life swells up inside us and overflows, there is no one to say "thank you" to excepting to God. The primitive symbol of "man in adoration," a stick person with arms stretched out to the skies, is a symbol of our recognition of, and gratitude to, God.

That's why thankfulness and the very sentiment of gratitude must be an embarrassment for the professing atheist. Who does he or she thank when feeling so profoundly grateful for the gift of life or love? Chuck Colson, in his autobiographical *Born Again*, tells of such a moment. He was teaching his ten-year-old son to sail.

---

[40] Robert Browning, "Bishop Blougram's Apology," , I, 313 in *Poems of Robert Browning*, Henry Frowde, London, Edinburgh, Glasgow, New York, Toronto, 1905, p. 139.

As the craft edged away from the dock, the only sound was the rippling of water under the hull and the flapping of the sail when puffs of wind fell from it. I was in the stern watching the tiller, Chris in the centre, dressed in an orange slicker, holding the sheet. As he realized that he was controlling the boat, the most marvellous look came over his cherubic face, the joy of new discovery in his eyes, the thrill of feeling the wind's power in his hands. I found myself in that one unforgettable moment quietly talking to God. I even recall the precise words: "Thank You, God, for giving me this son, for giving us this one wonderful moment...."

Afterwards, I had been startled when I realized that I had spoken to God, since my mind did not assent to His existence as a Person. It had been a spontaneous expression of gratitude that simply bypassed the mind and took for granted what reason had never shown me. More—it assumed that personal communication with this unproven God was possible. Why else would I have spoken, unless deep down I felt that Someone, somewhere, was listening?[41]

There is something admirable but very, very sad in the lines written by Sir Leslie Stephen after his wife's death. "I thank . . ." he began, and then remembering he had no God to thank, went on rather lamely, "I thank—something—that I loved her as heartily as I know how to love."[42]

And, of course, most of us will call upon God in the face of death. We accept death not willingly, but of necessity. We are creators of our history, conscious of infinitude, and therefore we find difficulty in accepting the annihilation of the self. But we are creatures of the history we create, subject to the vicissitudes of nature and the reality of our own mortality. We are meat, preserved by the miracle of life, but without the life, meat spoils and rots.

Though the fear of death may not be a universal phenomenon, it is common enough. In the ancient words of Cephalus, the aged father of Polemarchus, in the opening chapter of Plato's *Republic*:

---

[41] Charles W. Colson, *Born Again*, Bantam Books, New York, 1977, p. 134.
[42] Noted by Paul Scherer, *Facts That Undergird Life*, Harper and Brothers Publishers, New York and London, 1938, p. 178.

> I can tell you, Socrates, that, when the prospect of dying is near at hand, a man begins to feel some alarm about things that never troubled him before. He may have laughed at those stories they tell of another world and of punishments there for wrongdoing in this life. But now the soul is tormented by a doubt whether they may not be true. Maybe from the weakness of old age, or perhaps now that he is nearer to what lies beyond, he begins to get some glimpses of it himself. At any rate he is beset with fear and misgiving. He begins thinking over the past: is there anyone he has wronged? If he finds that his life has been full of wrongdoing, he starts up from his sleep in terror like a child. His life is haunted by dark forebodings!

Our trouble is not that we are merely and naturally mortal, but that we seem to realize at a deep level that we are meant for immortality and have lost our claim on it. "In the fear of death, it is not merely the knowledge of our finiteness that is preserved, but also the knowledge of our infinity, of our being determined for eternity and of our having lost eternity," wrote Paul Tillich.[43]

These are all evidences of our human need of God. But there are deeper, less obvious indications of our need of God. Secular humanism does not account for:

1. our very human need for meaning,

2. the human capacity for self-transcendence,

3. and the indeterminate possibilities of human freedom.

Let us examine each of these more closely.

The Need for Meaning

> This world's not blot for us,
> Nor blank—it means intensely, and means good:
> To find its meaning is my meat and drink.[44]

Humanity has an insatiable thirst for meaning. It seems built-in.

---

[43] *The Shaking of the Foundations*, Charles Scribner's Sons, New York, 1948, p. 171.
[44] Robert Browning, *Fra Lippo Lippi*, I, 313 in *Poems of Robert Browning*, Henry Frowde, London, Edinburgh, Glasgow, New York, Toronto, 1905, p. 129.

To live is to act. To act is to decide. Each decision we make represents a choice, one thing over another. We value *this* more than *that*. These values give meaning to our lives. We aspire to that which we value—to possess the things we count most valuable and to become what we admire. Behind these values is an understanding, a philosophy, of life.

Each of us in our living develops, more or less consciously, such a philosophy of life. Behind our formal, espoused beliefs and actions, there is a more basic belief and value system, one that guides our conduct and directs our lives. What we choose to do and be is dependent upon these convictions we hold about the meaning and the purpose of life, a "philosophy of life." From this we form a "standard of values," which determines what we work for and how we behave.

A philosophy of life and standard of values are not things we may choose to have, or choose not to have. They are built into our being, our humanity, and are essential by the very fact of living and acting and choosing. Our philosophy of life and standard of values, however, are not always consciously developed and held. With many people, they are largely unconscious and undeveloped. Nevertheless, even in the person who appears most thoughtless and uncaring, they still determine to a large extent the things we do and the things we aspire to do and to be—that which gives meaning to our lives.

The word "meaning" comes from the ancient Indo-European base *men,* meaning "think," possibly also the source of the word "man."[45] "Man (sic) is only a reed," wrote Pascal, "the weakest thing in nature, but he is a thinking reed."[46] It is by our capacity for thought that we are able to sort and compare, to put facts in categories and relate them one to another, and to choose one thing over another. So we reveal our values.

---

[45] John Ayto, *Dictionary of Word Origins*, Arcade Publishing, New York (Little Brown and Company), 1990,p. 343.

[46] Blaise Pascal, *Pensées, vi.*347, Great *Books of the Western World*, Robert Maynard Hutchins, Editor in Chief, Encyclopaedia Britannica, Inc., William Benton, Publisher, Chicago, London, Toronto, Geneva, Sydney, Tokyo, Manila, 1952 (Twenty-third printing, 1980), p. 233.

This ability to order, to categorize, to put things in their places, to arrange and use them, to "have dominion," is a mark of our humanity (as I kept telling my children in an effort to get them to keep their rooms tidy). Of course, this capacity is found to some extent in animals, even insects, but as far as we can know, it is not to the extent of the self-conscious decision making capability of human beings.

And because we can categorize and perceive distinctions, we can also see relationships between facts and things—even people, as we refer to our "relatives." To "relate" is to compare one thing with another, to see a pattern emerge from a mass of data or facts, to discern a meaning in the midst of apparent chaos. The word "relate" comes from a Latin root meaning to refer, to see how one matter refers back to another. For this reason we can see and can tell stories. We speak of "relating" a narrative. These stories indicate how we are able to discern meaning in our experiences, in our living. Douglas Coupland (to whom we referred) writes,

> One factor that sets us apart from all other animals is that our lives need to be stories—narratives—and that when our stories vanish, we feel lost, dangerous, out of control and susceptible to the forces of randomness. I call the process whereby one loses one's life-story "denarration."[47]

The need for meaning is built into our humanity. Quoting Paul Tillich,

> Man (sic) is more than an apparatus for registering so-called "facts" and their interdependence. He has to *know*, to know about himself as thrown into being, to know about the powers and structures controlling this being in himself and in his world. He wants to know the meaning of being because he is man and not an epistemological subject. Therefore he transcends and always must transcend the "No trespassing" signs cautiously built by scepticism and dogmatically guarded by pragmatism. The meaning of being is his basic concern, it is the really human and philosophical question.[48]

---

[47] Douglas Coupland, "Brentwood," *New Republic*, 19 December, 1994, quoted by Christopher Yates, "Hope for the Denarrated Self: Revisiting a Decade of Douglas Coupland," op. cit., p. 4.

[48] Tillich, *The Protestant Era*, p. 87.

But we human beings are not only able to think about things, we are able to think about ourselves. We possess self-consciousness and self-transcendence.

The Reality of Self-Transcendence

> The human spirit in its depth and height reaches into eternity and this vertical dimension is more important for the understanding of our humanity than merely our rational capacity for forming general concepts.[49]

We not only have this capacity to categorize, to order things around us, but also the capacity for the self to stand outside itself, to be conscious of its existence within time and space. Theologian Reinhold Niebuhr, back in the mid-twentieth century, wrote of humanity's capacity for self-transcendence, the ability of the self to make itself its own object.[50]

> The obvious fact is that man is a child of nature, subject to its vicissitudes, compelled by its necessities, driven by its impulses, and confined within the brevity of the years…. The other less obvious fact is that man is a spirit who stands outside of nature, life, himself, his reason and the world.[51]

Niebuhr makes particular reference to Augustine of Hippo's meditation on memory in his *Confessions*.[52] "The human memory is of particular importance to him as a symbol of man's (sic) capacity to transcend time and finally himself."[53] Our ability to remember things of the past suggests that we are not just creatures

---

[49] Reinhold Niebuhr, *Human Nature*. Vol. 1 of *The Nature and Destine of Man,* Nisbet & Co. Ltd., London, first published in 1941, reprinted March, 1949, p. 168.

[50] "If one turns to the question of the value of human life, … the very character of the question reveals that the questioner must in some sense be able to stand outside of, and to transcend, the life which is thus judged and estimated." Ibid., p. 2. Niebuhr seems to use the word in a theological sense of standing over or apart rather than the Kantian sense as that which transcends his categories and is hence beyond experience.

[51] ibid., 3-4.

[52] *Confessions,* Book X, pgs. 17-18.

[53] Niebuhr, p. 166.

of time. Our ability to "see" ourselves in a particular place indicates that we are not simply creatures of space. We have intimation of that which is beyond time and space. Because I am aware of myself sitting in this room on this particular Monday morning, I possess the capacity to be an object of my own regard.

Because I am able to stand outside of time and space, my knowledge, even my self-knowledge, is not confined to time and space.[54] We use words like "spirit" to allude to that which is not of space, and "eternity" to indicate that which is other than time. We may not know exactly what we mean by these words, but they do have meaning for us, or else we wouldn't use them.

> The common source of error of humanistic understandings of humanity is that they do not measure humanity in a dimension sufficiently high or deep to do full justice to either its stature or capacity for good or evil, or to understand the total environment in which such a stature can understand, express, and find itself....
>
> This total environment involves both time and eternity, and eternity cannot be known through the logical ordering of human experience. Humanity is thus in a position of being unable to comprehend itself in its full stature of freedom without a principle of comprehension which is beyond its comprehension.[55]

Niebuhr also saw the human capacity for self-transcendence as being without limit, indeterminate. I can be conscious of myself in this place and time, but I can also be conscious of myself being conscious of myself being conscious of myself, theoretically without limit.

In other words, we are such creatures as have some consciousness of infinitude, of eternity, and "our hearts are restless until ..." Until what? Until they find their peace with God.

Attempts to understand our own humanity have been among the greatest failures and faults of the twentieth century. We have made much progress in understanding our physical structure. We

---

[54] "As a creature who is involved in flux but who is also conscious of the fact that he is so involved, he cannot be totally involved. A spirit who can set time, nature, the world and being *per se* into juxtaposition to himself and inquire after the meaning of these things proves that in some sense he stand outside and beyond them" (Niebuhr, p. 133).

[55] Niebuhr, pp. 133-4.

have been much less successful in understanding our spiritual stature.

The Royal Society of London for Improving Natural Knowledge was formed in 1660, "a College for the promoting of Physico-Mathematicall Experimentall Learning."[56] The very recent Thirty-Year War saw terrible devastation and bloodshed, a pitting of Protestant against Roman Catholic and vice versa, a war, initially at least, fought over the Christian religion. European society had become disenchanted with "revealed religion" and with theology as "queen of the sciences." Many of the most knowledgeable people of the time were beginning to turn to "natural knowledge" and to the physical sciences for understanding of life and of human existence. In the 1730's, Alexander Pope published his "Essay on Man."

> Know then thyself; presume not God to scan,
> The proper study of mankind is man.[57]

In the twentieth century, a poet, Hugh Wilgus Ramsaur, would write,

> In desolation, here a lost world lies.
> All wisdom was its aim: with noble plan
> It sounded ocean deeps, measured the skies,
> And fathomed every mystery but Man![58]

The modem era has had great difficulty in finding the measure of our humanity. The tools and categories of "natural knowledge" have seemed inadequate to an understanding of ourselves. In the attempt to analyze our structure, we have forgotten the measure of our stature. But it's not by our structure that we take full measure of our humanity, but by our stature.

Structurally, we are puny creatures whose lives may be instantly ended by a falling stone or a flying bullet, or by an unseen virus, germ, or blood clot. Before the extent of the universe or the

---

[56] *The Encyclopaedia Britannica*, William Benton Publisher, Chicago, London, Toronto, etc. , 1967, Vol. 19, p. 674.

[57] *Masterpieces of Religious Verse*, ed. James Dalton Morrison, Harper and Brothers Publishers, New York and London, 1948, p. 273.

[58] ibid., 311.

power inherent in the atom, we are creatures infinitesimally small and weak, whose whole corporate existence and history may be obliterated in a second by worlds in collision or atoms in division.

It would take 1,300,000 planets the size of our earth to equal, roughly, the size of the sun. Yet, the sun is but one star in the galaxy of stars we call the Milky Way. Astronomers tell us there are not just millions, but trillions of other galaxies such as ours.

> O Lord, our Sovereign, how majestic is Your name in all the earth! ...
>
> When I look up into Your heavens, the work of Your fingers, the moon and the stars which you have created,
>
> What are human beings that You are mindful of them? (Psalm 8:1&3-4)

Structurally, we are like ants crushed by the heel of fate. But it's not structure that gives us significance; it's our stature.

We must recognize the reality of the universe, which overwhelms us. But before we allow ourselves to be overcome with a sense of our utter insignificance, we should think twice. Remember the words of Pascal, quoted earlier: "Man is only a reed, the weakest thing in nature, but he is a thinking reed." And he goes on, "By space the universe encompasses and swallows me as an atom; by thought, I encompass the universe."[59]

> After all, which is more marvellous, more indicative of what ultimate reality is like, the fact that the vast universe encompasses us, or the fact that man's mind so encompasses the vast universe, measures its distances, plots its laws? This is the critical juncture where man's varied philosophies meet and part, and the affirmation with which theistic faith begins is clear: *the mind that encompasses the universe is more marvellous and revelatory than the universe that encompasses the mind.*[60]

We cannot understand ourselves simply in terms of our empirical existence, our structure; we can only understand ourselves in terms of

---

[59] Pascal, Pensées, vi, 348, op. cit., p. 234.

[60] Harry Emerson Fosdick, *A Faith for Tough Times,* Harper and Brothers, New York, 1952, pp. 25-26. Emphasis mine.

our stature, our capacity for self-transcendence, our consciousness of the infinite and the eternal. We neglect this other dimension of our consciousness at the peril of our humanity. Consider the inhumanity of the twentieth century, which began with great hope and confidence of inevitable progress, and yet ended in apocalyptic gloom.

I have said that religion is not always a good thing. In fact, over the course of human history, religion has probably done more harm than good. It is important to humankind that we have religion that is true and good. But the reality remains that we are incurably religious. We are "created in the image of God." Created for relationship with the Eternal, "our hearts are restless till they find their rest in God." We need God and we will seek God in some form, in some way.

The Indeterminate Possibilities of Human Freedom

> The fact that man can transcend himself in infinite regression and cannot find the end of life except in God is the mark of his creativity and uniqueness: closely related to this capacity is his inclination to transmute his partial and finite self and his partial and finite values into the infinite good. Therein lies his sin.[61]

Freedom is a word we use often but seldom stop to think about. It is a word that has had great meaning in modern history, but is terribly misunderstood.

The Newtonian worldview has been powerfully influential in the understanding of our universe for the last 300 years. In this understanding, the world is self-contained, non-contingent. Within the system, there is no need of God. The Newtonian world gave us the watchmaker God, who made the universe as a carefully crafted watch, and then retired to the sidelines—in effect, retired.

Twentieth century physics discovered a whole new world of mysteries not explicable in terms of Newtonian physics. It is a world that is often non-quantifiable, where the distinction between

---

[61] Niebuhr, p. 131.

spirit and matter seems blurred and the limitations of physical science are more readily recognized. We have noted its inability to comprehend the full stature of our humanity.

Science also has been unable to understand the reality of freedom. Essentially science, at least Newtonian science, is deterministic. All is determined by cause and effect.[62] By the late nineteenth century, Charles Darwin advanced his theory of biological determinism and Karl Marx proposed a social (historical) determinism. It remained only for Sigmund Freud to claim that the actions of any individual were not primarily the result of a conscious process of reason and will but rather of impulses and compulsions rising out of the unconscious. Eliphaz, one of Job's comforters in Archibald MacLeish's play *J.B*, put it cogently:

> Science knows now that the sentient spirit
> Floats like a chambered nautilus on a sea
> That drifts it under skies that drive:
> Beneath the sea of the unconscious;
> Above the winds that wind the world.
> Caught between that sky, that sea,
> Self has no will, cannot be guilty.
> The sea drifts. The sky drives.
> The tiny, shining bladder of the soul
> Washes with wind and wave, or shudders
> Shattered between them.[63]

Christian faith itself has faced, down through all its centuries, the debate between those who argued for "freedom of the will" on the one hand, and those who advocated "predestinarianism" on the other hand. Determinism is the naturalistic equivalent of predestinarianism—the former being the scientific understanding that we are determined by natural law, the latter being the theological affirmation that we are predestined by God.

---

[62] "If the effort is made to comprehend the meaning of the world through the principle of natural causation alone, the world is conceived in terms of a mechanistic coherence which has no place for the freedom which reveals itself in human consciousness." Niebuhr, op. cit. p. 176.

[63] Archibald MacLeish, *J.B.: A Play in Verse*, Houghton Mifflin Company, Boston, The Riverside Press, Cambridge, 1956, Scene 9, p. 122-3.

The theological question, put simply, is this: How does one affirm the sovereignty and omnipotence of God and at the same time affirm human freedom? If God is all-powerful, how can it be said that we are free? But if human freedom is real, how can faith claim that God is omnipotent?

On the horns of this dilemma, Christian faith has tried to find ease by resting its understanding on one point or the other. The dilemma was glibly resolved by Samuel Johnson when he said to Boswell, his friend and biographer, "All thought favours determinism, and all experience is against it ... We know our will free, and there's an end on't."[64] Perhaps the old teetotaller of London's best days was right on.

We have indicated the human capacity of thought to compare and relate, to order and categorize, the things of the world around us, but there is a marvellous dynamism in life that, it would seem, cannot be comprehended in rational terms. Mathematics cannot comprehend motion. It can only understand movement as a series of points. We cannot, scientifically, understand the mystery of life itself. We have to kill it to analyze and dissect it. But then, all we understand is the working of a mechanism, not the life of an organism.

When we seek to treat freedom as something apart from our own subjectivity and experience, we lose the reality of it. When we think about or study freedom, we make it an object of our study or thought, and objects cannot be free. Freedom cannot be understood finally by our reason, by thought. It can only be experienced. Even one who claims to be a complete determinist, denying any human freedom, will still act in personal life as if freedom is a reality.

Our modern life is lived on these two levels: a scientific level in which freedom is denied (and as a result, human responsibility is reduced), and the popular or personal level in which we act as if freedom is real. The former has influenced our legal system, our philosophies, and humanities.[65] Yet we act, normally and necessarily,

---

[64] Boswell's *Life of Johnson,* Vol. II, p. 82, 16 October, 1769.
[65] Myer Levin's *Compulsion* , a fictionalized account of the Leopold-Loeb murder case of the 1920's, claimed that Clarence Darrow's defense was based on determinism, that the murder was an act of compulsion not of human freedom.

as if we are free, and we feel responsible, and often guilty, for our actions.

The human capacity for self-transcendence is the basis of our human freedom. As self-conscious beings, we can see ourselves and therefore, to some extent, can change ourselves. We see ourselves in our external circumstances, and so we can change our circumstances. The first requirement of social change is what Paulo Freire called "conscientiziation,"[66] a raising or realization of consciousness.

Because we are free, we can respond rather than just react. We are *response-able.* Further, because our self-transcendence is theoretically without limit, indeterminate, we have a sense of ultimate responsibility, responsible not just to others, but to God. This is what I understand it means to be created "in the image of God." We are created for responsible relationship with our Creator, our "heavenly Father," the One Jesus called Abba. Again, this is built into our humanity, no matter how fervently we try to deny it.

We are responsible for each other—and deep down we know it. The old stories still bear their truth. "Where is your brother, Abel?" God said to Cain, and Cain replied, "I do not know. Am I my brother's keeper?" (Genesis 4:1-16.) In spite of our Cain-like jealousy and anger, in spite of our fear of such immense responsibility, we know the answer is "Yes," we are our brothers' and sisters' keeper.

Whether or not we acknowledge God, we seem to know we are responsible for the care of this good earth on which we live. Note our vast ecological concern. The ancient creation story of the Hebrew people, unique among the various myths of creation, says that God gave humankind responsibility for creation. The word used in Genesis 1:26, usually translated "dominion," describes a standing over, a control of the world of nature. But in the context of the Biblical understanding of man and nature, it must be understood in terms of a special human responsibility for the world, to till and care for the garden God has given (Genesis 2:15).

---

[66] For an excellent short summary, see Gustavo Gutierrez, *A Theology of Liberation: History, Politics and Salvation,* translated and edited by Sister Caridad Inda and John Eagleson, Orbis Books, Maryknoll, New York, 1973, pp. 91-2.

> Man (sic) must remember that he is lord of creation and ruler of
> nature not in his own right or to work his own will; he is God's
> vice-regent, charged with the working of God's will, responsible
> to God for his stewardship. Otherwise his science and industry
> will bring not a blessing but a curse; they will make of the earth
> not a paradise but a dust-bowl or a Hiroshima.[67]

Humanity, through greed and fear, has continually ravished and
plundered the earth, turning gardens into deserts, perhaps
especially in the modern era when our power to do so has been
greater than ever before. We have been given this good earth not
only to use for our own benefit. We are also responsible for its
care, even for "all sheep and oxen, and also the beasts of the field,
the birds of the air, and the fish of the sea, and whatsoever passes
along the paths of the sea" Psalm 8:7-8). Our freedom involves a
sense of responsibility, even ultimate responsibility, from which
we cannot escape. We cannot escape from God.

No Need of That Hypothesis?

"Sire, I have no need of that hypothesis," Pierre Simon de Laplace is
reported to have replied to Napoleon Bonaparte after Bonaparte had
remonstrated with him for writing such a huge book (*Mécanique
Céleste*) without mentioning the Author of the universe. Whether
one can understand celestial mechanics without reference to God, it
would seem that human society cannot exist without its deities. In
Voltaire's famous phrase, "If God did not exist, it would be necessary to invent him."[68]

In my own life, I came to a place where it seemed to me that
either life was meaningless and purposeless, and happiness and love
and all that we valued were just illusions, or else at the centre of life
beat the heart of the loving God whom Jesus called Abba, "Father."

---

[67] Alan Richardson, *Genesis I-XI: Introduction and Commentary*, SCM Press, 56
Bloomsbury Street, London, WC1, 1953, p. 55. For an intelligent discussion of the
meaning of "dominion," see John C. L. Gibson, *The Daily Study Bible, Genesis,
Volume I*, The Saint Andrews Press, Edinburgh, The Westminster Press, Philadelphia,
1981, pp. 77-82.

[68] *Épitre à l'Auteur du Livre des Trois Imposteurs*, xcvi (November 10, 1770).

For me, it was that kind of either/or. I could not accept that life had no meaning, for then even this sentence I am writing would be meaningless. Somehow, then, I must try to understand the meaning of life as I see it in the Spirit of God, revealed in Jesus.

My answer to the question, "Do we really need God?" is still emphatically, enthusiastically, and urgently, "Yes, we really do need God." There are times when our need of God is obvious and real—in times of personal crisis, mortal peril, or national disaster, when we feel grateful or when we feel guilty, and in the face of death. There is the deeper evidence (the need for meaning, the reality of self-transcendence, and the indeterminate possibilities of human freedom) that indicate that we really do need God, and that we cannot long preserve our humanity without a sense of divinity.

> O weariness of men who turn from GOD
> To the grandeur of your mind and the glory of your action,
> To arts and inventions and daring enterprises,
> To schemes of human greatness thoroughly discredited,
> Binding the earth and the water to your service,
> Exploiting the seas and developing the mountains,
> Dividing the stars into common and preferred,
> Engaged in devising the perfect refrigerator,
> Engaged in working out a rational morality,
> Engaged in printing as many books as possible,
> Plotting of happiness and flinging empty bottles,
> Turning from your vacancy to fevered enthusiasm
> For nation or race or what you call humanity;
> Though you forget the way to the Temple,
> There is one who remembers the way to your door.[69]

---

[69] T. S. Eliot, *The Complete Poems and Plays 1909-1950*, Harcourt, Brace and World, Inc., New York, 1952, Choruses from "The Rock" III, p. 104.

THE GOD WE WANT AND THE GOD WE NEED

The God We Want

We have asked the question, "Do we really need God?" And we have answered, "Yes, we do. Humanity is incurably religious, and if we cannot find God, we will invent gods." And we do. Humanity seems to have a great capacity for creating gods. Many people have begun to realize that no-god is better than bad religion, and, as we have said, much religion is bad religion. Yet religion springs eternal from the human heart. And not all religion is bad religion. Religion can be good. It can comfort and strengthen, restrain wild impulses and self-destructive tendencies, and inspire greatness in common people.

Most bad religion results from our tendency to create gods to serve us. These are the gods we want. They are not the gods we need. When we create gods that will serve us, they end up controlling us rather than serving us. These gods are unpredictable and even malicious. Notice how many images of pagan gods are ugly and fearsome. Next, we seek ways to control these gods that we have created to get what we want from them. We bargain. We seek to placate. We pray fierce prayers. We offer sacrifices, sometimes even human sacrifices.

Two stories of Jacob in the Old Testament illustrate the difference between the gods we want and the God we need. Jacob and Esau were twins, with Jacob, the second born, grasping Esau's heel in birth. Hence he was named "Jacob," meaning the usurper or the grabber (Genesis 25:26).

In one (Genesis 27:41-28:22), Jacob, the "usurper," gained, through trickery and with his mother's connivance, the father's blessing and the birthright (the right of primogeniture) belonging to his older brother, Esau. In fear of Esau's wrath, he fled from his brother and spent the first night away from home on a hilltop with a stone for a pillow. There he had a wonderful dream in which God made Jacob an unconditional promise: "The land on which you lie I shall give to you and to your offspring, and your offspring shall be as the dust of the earth. ... Know that I am with you and will keep you wherever you go." Jacob realizes the presence of God, "Surely the Lord is in this place." The next morning, Jacob piled stones to make a pillar or cairn to mark the place. He named it Bethel, meaning "the house of God." Then he made a vow—but Jacob, ever wily, set down his conditions: "*If* God will be with me and keep me, and will keep me in this way that I go, and will give me bread to eat and clothing to wear, ... then the Lord shall be my God."

Here is the god that we want—a god who will serve us and give us our desires. Religion is so much more acceptable to people when it is a matter and means of getting God's attention and directing God's power to our service.

A few chapters later (Genesis 31f.), much has happened to Jacob. He has served his uncle, Laban, hard and long. He has married twice and become the head of a large contingent of children, servants, and beasts. After serving Laban for over twenty years, with much conflict, and evidently much mutual deception, Jacob decides to return "home," to the land of his fathers.

But, of course, waiting for him at home is the wronged brother, Esau. Jacob, remembering how he had cheated and mistreated his brother, was afraid. When messengers returned to tell him that Esau was coming to meet him with four hundred men, "Jacob was greatly afraid and distressed." He made elaborate preparations for the encounter, dividing all who were with him, including flocks and herds and camels, into two companies so that if Esau came upon one and destroyed it, the other might escape.

Then Jacob prayed, an earnest prayer, a humble prayer. "I am not worthy...! Deliver me, I pray, from the hand of my brother, from the hand of Esau, for I fear him." He then prepared a lavish present for his brother, goats and sheep and camels, and sent them on ahead, dividing them into groups with spaces in between and instructing his servants to tell Esau that these were a present and that Jacob was following. "For he thought, 'I may appease him with the present that goes before me, and afterwards I shall see his face; perhaps he will accept me.'"

Finally, he took his two wives and two concubines and his eleven children and sent them on ahead. Left alone, at the ford of the Jabbok River, he wrestled through the night with a "man" who left him crippled but undefeated. And the man (or angel) blessed Jacob and said, "Your name shall no more be called Jacob (usurper), but Israel, for you have striven with God and with men, and have prevailed." (The name, Israel, means "one who strives with God").

The God who met him here in his loneliness and desperation was not the God he wanted, but a God who forced him to struggle, confronting him with himself and with his past, and leaving him marked for life. But this was the God Jacob needed. Here, he became "Israel," no longer a usurper, but a prince, father of the people who came to be known as "the children of Israel."

For the God of the Bible is not the God we want, one who serves us, but the One who created us and whose creatures we are, to whom we owe our life and all that we have. But this is also the One who questions us and challenges us and calls us to respond, and who calls us to a life of service, of Him and of others, and to the stewardship of creation.[70]

We have pointed to the human capacity of self-transcendence, a consciousness of ourselves within time and space and therefore a capability of transcending time and space. As we can see ourselves, so we can change ourselves. We are free, able to make choices based on a more or less consciously held standard of values. These values give meaning to our lives. They point to our religion—for whatever our formal profession, our religion is what we do with our living, what we live for, whether that be family, money, power, love, or acceptance. Because we are conscious of ourselves within the immense forces of nature and the seemingly chance concatenations of circumstance, we turn for help to others, to loved ones, even to those spirits or gods which we think lurk behind and within the reality apparent around us.

---

[70] There are, of course, many examples in the Bible of people who want to use God for their private purposes, but the uniqueness of the Biblical witness is the One who demands of us our service, our loyalty.

Idolatry

On a mission project in Japan, my wife and I were invited to a home where the grandfather was the only Christian. I asked him what it meant to him to be a Christian. He replied that a Christian was one who didn't smoke or drink or swear. I turned to the non-Christian son and asked him what it meant to be a Christian. He replied that he believed that we create God in our image, not that God created us in His image. I found the answer of the grandfather quite simplistic, quite moralistic. I'm afraid he got overlooked while the son and I had an intense discussion.

The son identified what idolatry is. We create the gods we want. We create God in our image.

The first two commandments of the Decalogue (the Ten Commandments) are concerned with idolatry.

The first, Exodus 20:3, says, "Thou shalt have no other gods before me." The second, Exodus 20:4, commands God's people not to make "any graven images." (Note also Deuteronomy 5:6-10.) The first implies that nothing shall be given pre-eminence over God—not money, not power, not pleasure, not fame. Nor should family or country come before our allegiance to God. This is the more subjective of the two commandments. The second, the prohibition of any "graven image" to represent God, is more objective.

The prohibition of "other gods" and "graven images" is prominent throughout the Hebrew scriptures. The post-Exilic prophet sometimes called "the second Isaiah," pokes fun at gods of gold, silver, or wood.

> *To whom then will you liken God,*
> *or what likeness compare with Him?*
> *The idol?—A workman casts it,*
> *and a goldsmith overlays it with gold*
> *and casts for it silver chains.*
> *He who is impoverished chooses for an offering*
> *wood that will not rot;*
> *He seeks out a skilled craftsman to set up*
> *an image that will not move (totter).*
> *Have you not known? Have you not heard?*
> *Has it not been told you from the beginning?*

Have you not understood from the foundations of the earth?
It is he who sits above the circle of the earth,
And its inhabitants are as grasshoppers;
who stretches out the heavens like a curtain,
and spreads them like a tent to dwell in.
(Isaiah 40:18-22.)

This is the first and the most primitive level of idolatry—images of wood, clay, silver, gold, etc. to represent the deity. Humanity seems to need some representation of its deities, whether idols or icons.

Why does the Hebrew scripture protest so vehemently "other gods" and "graven images?" To answer, let us consider the bull.

Around the ancient Mediterranean, from the Aegean to Canaanite religions, the bull was the common symbol of power and fecundity. The Canaanites were evidently the most populous of the peoples of the land in which the Israelites sought to settle. They were a people with an urban culture and also a rural population cultivating the land. In contrast, the Israelites were a nomadic people bound together by a strong religious faith, who swept in from the desert, harassing and marauding. Even when they settled and lived among the Canaanites, they didn't understand or greatly appreciate the culture and had little knowledge of the best land to choose for cultivation or the best way to utilize it to grow the crops. The gods of the prosperous Canaanites must have seemed very attractive to the Israelites, especially as the worship of these gods seemed so free and easy in contrast to the laws, commandments, and all the restrictions required by their own God, Yahweh. The whole purpose of the Canaanite religion was to get the gods to serve you, to make you prosperous and powerful.

Nature and fertility religions, as the Canaanite religion was, are cyclical, following the order of the seasons. The central god of the Canaanite pantheon was the Baal, often represented as a bull. One of the myths of the Baal claimed that each year, after the months of drought, the rains would return (understood as the semen of Baal), falling upon the earth, and the earth goddess would again produce the crops by which people lived. Thus, the rituals of fertility religions involved a lot of sex or sacred prostitution, no doubt a good way to get people to "go to church."[71]

Little wonder that the Israelite people were attracted to Canaanite religion. But by their own religion, they maintained their identity not only as Israelites but also as a people specially chosen by God to enter into a covenant, a special relationship, with Yahweh.

Canaanite religion typifies much human religion. So much human religiosity, in fact I am tempted to say almost all human religiosity, seeks a god who will give people what they want.

The word "idol" is not a Hebrew word. The Hebrew scriptures use terms like "graven image" (sculptured) or "molten image" (made from a mould). The word "idol" comes from the Greek *eidos*, meaning any form or shape. Its Latin derivative, *idolum*, refers to an image of a false god.

Eugene Peterson defines idolatry as "reducing God to a concept or object that we can use for our benefit," and says it is "endemic to the human condition."[72] Of course, we are now not talking about "graven images" or things made with hands. We are recognizing that idols can be the product of our minds. It is significant that our word "idea" comes from the same root as "idol."[73] This is the second level of idolatry.

"We are not made in God's image, instead we make God in our image," said the young man in Japan. He was echoing a common thought, perhaps most forcefully expressed by Ludwig Feuerbach, the nineteenth century German described by Karl Barth as an anti-theologian,[74] who taught that "man's essential being" was "the measure of all things and in which he thought he saw man's true divinity." He believed religion to be the mirror of man's own nature and God, or the gods, merely the product of

---

[71] This is a rather simplistic account of a complex reality but which I trust is true in its general outline.

[72] Eugene Peterson, *Christ Plays in Ten Thousand Places: A Conversation in Spiritual Theology*, William B. Eerdmans Publishing Company, Grand Rapids, MI, 2005, p. 29-30.

[73] John Ayto, *Dictionary of Word Origins*, Arcade Publishing, New York, 1990. p. 203.

[74] "Feuerbach was an outsider; not a theologian, but a philosopher engaging in theology…. In effect, what he practiced was anti-theology." Karl Barth, *Protestant Thought from Rousseau to Ritschl*, Harper and Brothers, New York, 1959, p. 355.

human creativity. Feuerbach wanted, says Karl Barth, to turn theology "completely and finally into anthropology."[75]

In one sense, Feuerbach was right. This is what we do. We want a god who is "user friendly," who will provide for our needs and desires and shower us with blessings.[76] This is the god we want, and we will strive to develop technologies and systems that will do just that, whether animal or human sacrifice or the free market system.

Creating gods in our image does not mean just creating images in human or animal form, whether sculpted of clay or gold or silver or painted on the ceiling of the Sistine Chapel. It means also the creations of our minds, that to which we give ultimate or divine power or significance, the human parading as the divine, the relative as the absolute, the penultimate as the ultimate. Creating God in our image happens when human systems take on pretensions of being the Kingdom of God. In the long run, it doesn't work.

Reinhold Niebuhr pointed out why creating god in our image doesn't work:

> Man, who is made in the image of God is unable, precisely because of those qualities in him which are designated as "image of God," to be satisfied with a god who is made in man's image.[77]

The Final Idolatry

The final idolatry is when we worship our religion, or have faith in our faith, rather than recognizing that God is always more than our conception of God.

---

[75] Barth, note pp. 355-361.

[76] The word "bless" is found only in the English language, meaning originally "marked with blood." (Note Ayto, p. 67.) It was used to translate the Latin *benedicere* and the Hebrew *bahruch*. "The only constant connotations of 'blessed' is well-being, prosperity, which is the gift of God to man." (Note *The Interpreter's Dictionary of the Bible*, Abingdon Press, New York/Nashville, 1962, Vol. I, pp. 445-6.) In the New Testament, those who are blessed are those who suffer for their faith, hence "marked with blood."

[77] Niebuhr, *Human Nature*, chp. 6, p. 177.

In religion, too, we must keep a critical attitude that never unconditionally accepts any socially established form of revelation. Otherwise, we are back to idolatry again, this time a self-idolatry rather than an idolatry of nature, where devotion to God is replaced by the deifying of our own present understanding of God. The apostle Paul tells us that we are God's temples: if so, we should be able to see the folly of what was proposed by the Emperor Caligula for the Jerusalem temple, of putting a statue of ourselves in its holy place.[78]

This "deifying of our own present understanding of God" is evident not only in much human religion, but also much of the Christian religion. For example, Tomas de Torquemada of the Spanish Inquisition was an ascetic, a thoroughly righteous man in his own understanding and very religious, and he was supremely confident in the righteousness of his cause. In another instance, and from another point of view, Oliver Cromwell wrote to the General Assembly of the Church of Scotland (August 3, 1650), challenging their confidence in their own righteousness: "I beseech you, in the bowels of Christ, think it possible you may be mistaken."[79]

This idolatry of our religion, our cause, is most evident in times of strife. We consider God to be on our side and label our enemies an axis of evil. *We* are right and *they* are wrong. Abraham Lincoln, in the midst of the American Civil War, pointed out that both sides "read the same Bible and pray to the same God, and each invokes His aid against the other."[80] The words of Paul to the church at Rome apply not only to individuals but also to governments, nations, councils, and churches: "There is none righteous, no not one" (Romans 3:10).

The deadly thing about the gods we want and the idols we create is the way they turn on us and bite us, ensnaring us so we become slaves of the very gods who were to serve and save us. Take two examples: the family and nation/race.

---

[78] Northrop Frye, *The Double Vision: Language and Meaning in Religion*, The United Church Publishing House, Toronto, Canada, 1991, pp. 38-39.

[79] Though, no doubt, Cromwell was equally confident of the righteousness of his own cause.

[80] Second Inaugural Address, March 4, 1865.

Take first the family, surely one of the greatest blessings given by God. The purpose of the family surely is to provide a reasonably limited and safe environment in which children can learn to love—first their mother and father, then siblings, then playmates and friends, and finally learn the love of neighbour and possibly eventually the love of enemies.[81]

But when the family becomes an end in itself and thus an idol, society breaks down into tribalism, the kind of inter-tribal warfare we see happening today, not only in Africa and other far places, but also in our culture. We see concern for the common good lost among competing interests—professional organizations and unions, and sadly not least, among political parties whose primary concern should be the common good but who seem to chiefly strive to hold on to power.

We may take the motto of the Mafia as an example: "the family is our thing" (*cosa nostra*). The "Don" looks after the welfare of his "family," and to hell with everybody else.

In the same way as we have considered the family, consider race and nation, blood and soil. These also are gifts of God, but when they become idols they wreak much havoc and destruction. Remember Nazism.

There is a legend that the ancient kings of Europe, going down into the waters in Christian baptism, held their sword arm out of the water, a kind of conditional acceptance of Christian faith that would allow them still to use the sword—and the soil of the nations of Europe has been stained with the blood of thousands upon thousands of their sons ever since.

These human things, given the attributes of deity, become demonic forces in human society. The gods, created by human ingenuity, soon become tyrants and their devotees become their slaves. Money and power, when they become the end purpose of our living, become a kind of addiction that diminishes the human-

---

[81] Note Ephesians 3:14-15, which intimates that fatherhood and family life is patterned on the Fatherhood of God. The great New Testament scholar, James Moffatt, who provided a "new translation" of the Bible at the beginning of the 20th century, translated this passage, "I bow my knees before the Father, from whom every family in heaven and on earth derives its name and nature." (*The New Testament: a New Translation*, London, Hodder and Stoughton, 1913, p. 292.)

ity of those who choose to serve them. Family and nation, when they are more important than the kingdom of God, become demonic. The human creature, who was their creator and who gave them ultimate status, becomes their creature. The gods we have created to serve us, the gods we want, become lords over us (the word Baal means "lord") and we become their slaves.

The Lord

Of course, not only pagan gods have names. The God of Israel also has a name. We can't be sure how to say it, because ancient scribes copying the manuscripts which have come to form our Bible, out of reverence, wrote only the four consonants: YHWH. They omitted the vowels. It was the name given to Moses (Exodus 3:13-14), usually translated as "I AM," but was held in such reverence by the Israelites that it was never uttered. Scholars' best guess is YaHWeH. It was translated by the Greek word *kyrios* (lord) when the Hebrew scriptures were translated into the Greek language about 270 BC, and so has passed over into English usage as "lord."

The Baal was also called lord, but the understanding of lordship in the Hebrew scriptures (and also in the New Testament) was quite different. Whereas Yahweh promised little to his people other than to be with them and make them a great nation, Baal promised what the people wanted—prosperity and plenty. But the result of the worship of Baal ended in subjugation and oppression to the god and the social system. The worship of Yahweh resulted in a social order more free and yes, I believe, fulfilling (if not necessarily prosperous), for the Hebrew people.

In the early Christian church, Jesus soon was understood as "the Lord." At first, the disciples began to call Jesus "Rabbi," teacher. Then they began to wonder if Jesus might be the Messiah, the Promised One, a suspicion confirmed by Peter's confession, "You are the Christ (Messiah)" (e.g. Mark 8:29). After the resurrection appearances, there seems to be a new understanding and the word takes on new meaning. Thomas, confronted with the nail-holes in the hands and the spear-hole in the side of the body of the risen Christ, is recorded as crying out, "My Lord and my God!" (John 20:28). The apostle Paul speaks repeatedly of Jesus as "the Lord." He quotes what is evidently an early Christian hymn, ending "every tongue confess that Jesus Christ is Lord" (note Philippians 2:5-11). The earliest Christian confession was evidently "Jesus is Lord."

In the Gospel of John, written slightly later than the other Gospels, in which Jesus' relationship to and identification with God is more explicit, Jesus is often called "Lord." Significantly, this Gospel also records Jesus as using the name of God, "I AM," to refer to himself: "I AM the bread of life" (John 6:35); "I AM the light of the world" (John 8:12); "I AM the resurrection and the life" (John 11:25); "I AM the way, the truth, and the life" (John 14:6). And in the earliest testimony, the Gospel of Mark, at His trial before the Sanhedrin, when Jesus is questioned by the high priest, "Are you the Messiah, the Son of the Blessed?" Jesus is reported as replying, "I AM" (Mark 14:62).

It seems obvious that the New Testament understands Jesus as the Lord, but gave a whole new meaning to the term "lord."

In John 13, meeting with the disciples just before His betrayal, trial, and crucifixion, Jesus took a basin and towel and washed the feet of His disciples, the work of a slave. "If I, your Lord and teacher, have washed your feet, you also ought to wash one another's feet" (John 13:14).

It is there through the Gospels.

> *You know that those who are supposed to rule over the Gentiles lord it over them, and their great men exercise authority over them. But it shall not be so among you, but whoever would be great among you must be our servant, and whoever would be first among you must be slave to all. For the Son of Man came not to be served, but to serve and to give his life as a ransom for many.* (Mark 10:42-45, J.B. Phillips translates this last phrase, "to set others free.")

Here we have a different understanding of lordship. It is an understanding not completely lost in our history. The word lord originally meant "guardian of the loaf,"[82] intimating the one responsible for the nurture and welfare of the community.

---

[82] Ayto, p. 328.

However, the lords of human history have commonly been of another breed, more concerned with the accumulation of personal wealth and power. Rather than a stewardship of office, a responsibility for their people, they have ended up exercising power over the people and using the people for their own personal power and wealth.

They are the gods we thought we wanted, but we have found our need is for another God, one who confronts us and challenges us as the stranger-in-the-night confronted Jacob, causing us to face ourselves and our faults. This is the God we know through the Bible, who called in the garden, "Adam, where are you?" (Genesis 3). In the wilderness to Moses, "Come, I will send you to Pharaoh" (Exodus 3). To Isaiah, "Who will I send?" (Isaiah 6) And by the shores of Galilee, "Follow me" (e.g. Mark 1:16-20).

I appeal to you, therefore, brothers and sisters, by the mercies of God, to present your bodies as a living sacrifice (Romans 12:1).

The God We Cannot Find
and the God We Cannot Escape

It seems that there is a God we seek and cannot find. There is also a God from whom we cannot escape. Together, they are one God, the same.

Take, for example, a story told of Willard Brewing, who was minister of St. Andrew's Wesley United Church in Vancouver in the mid-twentieth century. Following a Sunday morning service, one of the women of the church was fixing the flowers at the front of the church when she saw a small boy walking slowly down the great central aisle, looking around at the beautiful windows, the impressive chancel, and lifting wide eyes to the high vaulted ceiling of the sanctuary.

The woman turned as the lad came to the front of the church and asked him what he was looking for. The little fellow looked up at her with wide, solemn eyes and said, "I'm looking for God."

The woman naturally took the boy to see the minister, Dr. Brewing, who in turn asked him what he wanted. The lad replied again, "I'm here looking for God."

And Dr. Brewing, in grace and wisdom, replied, "Well, son, God is here, looking for you."

One place in the Bible, a man (Job) seeks God, but cannot seem to find Him.

> *I go forward, but God is not there; backward, but still I cannot see Him. On one hand I look, but God is not to be found; on the other, but there's no sign of Him.... Oh that I knew where I might find God that I might come into His presence* (Job 23:8-9, 3).

Here is the God we cannot find.

In contrast, we read the words of Psalm 139:

> *Where can I go from your Spirit?*
> *Where can I flee from your presence?*
> *If I ascend to heaven, you are there.*
> *If I make my bed in Sheol, you are there.*
> *If I take the wings of the morning*
> *and settle at the farthest limits of the sea,*
> *even there your hand shall lead me,*
> *your right hand shall hold me*
> (Psalm 139:7-12).

Here is the God we cannot escape.

But these are one God, one and the same—*the God we cannot find, and the God we cannot escape.*

THE GOD WE CANNOT FIND

We are so often like the little boy—looking for God. We seek a sense of God's presence, of God's grace and strength for our life. And our problem seems to be that we have so much trouble finding God.

This is, when you think of it, quite surprising. If God is God, and if God has created all that is, even created us in His own image so that "our hearts are restless till they find their rest in Him," then surely God should not be so difficult to find.

Yet this seeming inability to find God has led to the belief by some that there is no God (what we have come to call "atheism"), or at least that we cannot know whether God exists or what God is like (what we call "agnosticism"). This phenomenon is evidently rather unique to our time. Men and women of all times and races have been many things, both good and bad, but they have been religious. But in our day, in the words of T. S. Eliot,

> It seems that something has happened that has never happened
>   before:
> Though we know not just when, or why, or how, or where.
> Men have left God not for other gods, they say, but for no god:
>   and this has never happened before,
> That men both deny gods and worship gods, professing first
>   Reason,
> And then Money, and Power, and what they call Life, or Race, or
>   Dialectic.
> The Church disowned, the tower overthrown, the bells upturned,
>   what have we to do
> But stand with empty hands and palms turned upwards,
> In an age which advances progressively backwards?[83]

I have a lot of sympathy with the atheist or the agnostic because of my own struggle and search. God was once, for me, a pretty remote proposition. Certainly a thoughtful agnosticism seems preferable to the idolatry or superstition to which religion often tends.

And yet I find myself rather short of patience with the usual arguments about whether or not God exists, and with those who want some kind of proof about the whole thing. After all, God is not a created object, one thing among others, subject to the laws of empirical procedures. God is the One beyond, the Creator of all that is.

You don't find God like a lost coin. God is not lost.

How, after all, would you prove or disprove the existence of God? By science? Would you put God in a test-tube, add some kind of acid, and if there's a big puff of blue smoke you would know that God does exist?

Would you prove God's existence by logic? It is God who has given us minds to think with and created the kind of order in which the rules of logic and the categories of the mind operate.

You can't prove the existence of God. If you could, God's existence would then be subject to the proof, dependent upon our

---

[83] "Choruses from 'The Rock'" – VII, *The Complete Poems and Plays, 1909-1950*, Harcourt, Brace & World Inc., 1952, p. 108.

logic for His existence. And that would be patently ridiculous, for God would no longer be God.

When it comes to it, can you prove that anything exists? This is at the present time one of the central questions science is wrestling with: is there any method of verifiability that guarantees objective knowledge?

Can you "prove" that beauty exists? Or love? Or happiness? For that matter, can you prove that *you* exist?—Think about that! Wouldn't you just sputter around, and finally say, after a while, "Well, I *know* that I exist, and that's all there is to it."

I suppose the realization of our own existence is one of the chief reasons for believing in God. Because I am, therefore God is! I think this is a better summary of the philosophical system of Rene Descartes than the well known *Cogito ergo sum*, "I think, therefore I am." This was only Descartes' starting point. He was trying to demonstrate, to prove the existence of God. His own being, his own consciousness, led him to assume or conclude the existence of God.

One of the chief criticisms of Descartes' system is that it results in what is called "the egocentric predicament." In the end, you are sure that you exist, but you aren't sure that anything else exists. You end up cut off from all else in a little cell of self-centred self-consciousness, frightened and afraid. It's a true picture, when you think of it, of what the Bible calls the human state of "sin," and it's an amazing analysis of the self-centredness of our modern technological western society.

Have you noticed that the Bible never tries to prove the existence of God? It starts with God. "In the beginning, God created the heavens and the earth..." (Genesis 1:1). Instead of saying, "I am, therefore God is." The Bible says, "God is, therefore I am."

And it's exactly when we open the Bible and are confronted with the God revealed in its pages that we get a new perspective of our own problem with God. Our problem, I believe, is not that we cannot find God. Our problem is that we cannot escape from God.

THE GOD WE CANNOT ESCAPE

The problem, I say, is not that God is lost, like a coin or a sheep, and must be found. The problem is that *we* are lost, shut in the prison house of our egocentricity, our "egocentric predicament." We are like a girl who shuts her eyes and then complains that she cannot see. Like a man running from a tiger, all the while claiming that nothing is chasing them.

The reason we cannot find God is not because God is inaccessible, but because we have turned away from God and have tried to find meaning for life within ourselves. This is the sin of Adam, "to be as gods," to put ourselves at the centre of our existence where only God can be.

God's command is heavy—to love Him with all our heart and soul and strength and mind, and to love our neighbour as ourselves. In our self-concern, we are anxious and afraid that the fulfillment of God's command should be the annihilation of our own happiness, our security, and in fact, perhaps, our very selves. How will we survive if we are called to give ourselves away, in love?

We are so commonly aware of our search for God and our desire to be righteous. It's difficult for us to acknowledge, even to ourselves, our fear of God and our denial of God's commands.

I speak from my own experience. For several years, I engaged in "a spiritual search," searching for God, the sense of God's presence. When at last I came to a faith that was mine, I had the sense, not that I had found God, but that God had found me. Not that God had answered all my questions, but rather that God was demanding of me an answer, the answer of my life.

Repeatedly, in the Bible, it is God who does the seeking. It is God who asks the questions and demands an accounting. In the garden, in the cool of the day, "Adam, where are you?" (Genesis 3:9). Moses, hiding in the desert, and inexplicably a bush bursts into flame, and Moses cowers in the realization of God's presence and God's call—"Go down to Egypt" (Exodus 3).

Job cries, "O that I knew where I might find God and place my case before Him" (Job 23:3), but when God speaks to Job out of the whirlwind, He doesn't answer Job. Instead God asks questions of Job, demanding of him an accounting. The strange thing is that there, face to face with the Almighty, Job seems to find what he was looking for (Job 38f). *The God we cannot seem to find is, in reality, the God from whom we seek to escape and cannot.*

Remember that quotations from Psalm 139 a few pages back:

Where can I go from your Spirit?
Where can I flee from your Presence?
If I ascend to heaven, you are there.
If I make my bed in Sheol,
  you are there.
If I take the wings of the morning
  and settle at the farthest limits of the sea,
even there your hand shall lead me,
your right hand shall hold me.
If I say, "Surely the darkness shall cover me,
  and the light around me become night,"
  even the darkness is not dark to you;
  the night is as bright as the day,
for darkness is as light to you.
(Psalm 139:7-12)

One reason the Bible is either a book very deeply loved, or one which people would rather avoid, is it tells us that at the heart of the mystery of life is the One whom we fear most of all and before whom we feel strangely guilty but who, through searching, yearning, and His unending love, will never let us get finally and utterly away.

I fled Him, down the nights and down the days;
I fled Him down the arches of the years;
I fled Him down the labyrinthine ways
Of my own mind; and in the midst of tears
I hid from Him, and under running laughter.
Up vistaed hopes I sped,
And shot, precipitated,
Adown titanic glooms of chasmed fears
From those strong feet that followed, followed after.[84]

From almost the first moment of creation—God crying in the garden, "Adam, where are you?"—down through the long and dusty centuries, God has been seeking and wooing a rebellious people—"When Israel was a child, then I loved him and called my son out of Egypt" (Hosea 11:1)—even to this present time, to here and now, and me and you.

---

[84] Francis Thompson, *The Hound of Heaven*, pp. 5-6.

This is what the Bible is about, not our search for God but God's search for us, and our continuing attempts to escape from this diligent and demanding grace. This is the God who was in Jesus Christ, the shepherd who would go out into the darkness and the storm to seek and to save all who were lost.

> ... and none of the ransomed ever knew
> How deep were the waters crossed;
> Nor how dark was the night that the Lord passed through,
> E'er He found His sheep that was lost.[85]

This is what the cross is all about: the illimitable lengths to which God will go to seek and to save this lost and perishing race.

And don't you see? It was Jesus Himself who personified this same God—who in His person came to seek and to save the lost.

> *Let this mind be in you which was in Christ Jesus; who, being in glory with God, thought His glory not something to be clung to, but gave it up, and made Himself of no account. He was made in human form, and took on Himself the role of a servant. He humbled Himself, even to death—and the death He died was that of a common criminal!* (Philippians 2:5-8.)

A minister, new to his congregation and trying to get to know his people, rang the doorbell of a home where the wife attended church but the husband did not. The husband answered the door, explained his wife was not home, and went on to say to the minister, "I want you to know that I don't believe in God. I don't go to church, and I don't believe much that the church stands for." He went on to talk about injustice in life and hypocrisy in the church. When he had said his say, the minister replied,

> Let me tell you something that happened to me when I was a child. One day I did something bad, real bad. I was afraid that my parents would punish me, so I ran away and hid. I knew my parents would be worried, but I stayed away until well after dark and I was sure my parents would be in bed. Then, because I didn't have anywhere to go, I stole home, into the house, and upstairs to my bedroom. My folks had left a light on downstairs, but upstairs

[85] "The Ninety and Nine," by Elizabeth Cecilia Clephane, *The Hymnary of the United Church of Canada*, The United Church Publishing House, Toronto, 1930, No. 475.

was dark, and when I turned to go into my bedroom, I thought I saw a ghost. I turned and ran (all the time telling myself there was nothing there!) In my panic, I fell down the stairs and broke my leg and had to go around on a crutch for several months.

The other man looked puzzled by this story for a moment, but then a light dawned in his eyes and he said, "But there wasn't any ghost there." "No," said the minister, "what I thought was a ghost was, in reality, my father, waiting for me to come home."

The Only Way?

In the upper room, the night before He died, Jesus spoke words to His disciples which they would not forget. Among these, recorded years later in John's Gospel, are words that have caused much misunderstanding. As that Gospel records, Jesus said, "I am the way, the truth, and the life; no one comes to the Father but by me" (John 14:6).

Is Jesus saying, and am I saying, that only those who believe in Jesus Christ are saved? That all others are slated for eternal damnation?

No, of course not! To say this, we would have to cross out, expunge, obliterate, so much of the New Testament that there would not be much left. The whole idea does not accord with the Spirit of Jesus as recorded in the New Testament.

I cannot believe that the Gospel, the "good news," declares that those who have never heard the name of Jesus, through no fault of their own, should be damned eternally—millions upon millions down through the history of the human race, before Jesus as well as since. That stands up to neither scripture nor reason.

There are many others who do not own the name of Christian because Jesus Christ has been presented to them in a way not true to the Gospel. They were given an understanding of God and the Gospel that was hard, cruel, and partial to those who held a similar belief. If the preaching of some preachers on radio and television were all I knew or heard of the Gospel, I would never have become a Christian.

How often the proclamation of the Gospel has been hedged by false conditions on the grace of God. "Unless you go to the right church and receive the sacraments in the proper manner...!" "Unless you believe the Bible from cover to cover...!" "Unless you have the right kind of salvation experience...!" "Unless you are baptized by the Holy Spirit and speak in tongues...!" "Unless you truly and earnestly repent of your sins...! When can I say that I have "truly repented?"

These are all false conditions placed on the Gospel. How can we so narrowly circumscribe God's grace that "only me, my wife, and my son John" are going to be allowed into the presence of the heavenly Father? The word Gospel means "good news." There is not much here to call good news.

I understand this text not exclusively, but inclusively. It is not by naming the name that we know God, but by Word and Spirit. The Word of God through the Bible tells us of the love of God, and the Spirit of God stirs our hearts to respond, to say, "Yes, this is what God is like. This is what God must be like!"

Sometimes those who call themselves Christians exhibit by their very exclusiveness and self-righteousness a spirit foreign to the love of Christ. No matter how much we name the name of Jesus, if we do not see in Jesus this wonderful love, reaching out to all, we do not then recognize the Spirit of God. "Not everyone who says to me, 'Lord, Lord' will enter the Kingdom of heaven, but only the one who does the will of my Father in heaven" (Matthew 7:21).

The point of the Gospel is, first of all, not to convert people to Christianity, but to assure them of the inclusive, all-embracing love of God in Christ. The former is proselytizing, the latter evangelizing.[86] This love we know in Jesus is the expression of the Spirit of God. This Spirit is the only path to life, to true life, abundant life, and to justice, peace and human fulfillment. No number of words, in known or unknown tongues, no profession of faith, no matter how correct or orthodox, no amount of prayer, of pleading or piety, will lead us to the Father which is not of this

---

[86] Note Brian Stanley, "Conversion to Christianity: Colonization of the Mind?" *International Review of Mission*, Vol. XCII, No. 366, note pp. 322 f. Stanley argues that evangelization is not "a one-way process, in which the missionary endeavours to implant within the mind of the hearer a normative set of beliefs, i.e. a new 'religion' that replaces the previous one.... Conversion ... in the New Testament is not primarily about replacement but about the transformation and reorientation of humanity towards God."

Spirit of Jesus, this Spirit of love. For this Spirit is the life-giving Spirit by which the universe was formed and which is yet "the still point of the turning world."[87]

There is universality in the Spirit of Jesus Christ that defies narrow limitations. Our hearts rise up and say, "Yes" to that Spirit of love, which we see in Him. See, for instance, the way the human race, of all cultures and races, respond to the Spirit of Christmas which has become important in Japan as in Canada. We deep down know that this self-giving, sacrificial love, which we see in Jesus, is the very Spirit of God, and if we all lived in that Spirit, there would indeed be peace on earth and goodwill among all people.

"No one can come to the Father but by me!" Not by naming the name, but in the Spirit of *agape*, only in love and by love, can we know God. This is as inclusive as you can get. Anyone, regardless of name or place or race, of status or education, regardless of wealth or moral qualities, anyone can know God; not just those who own the name of Jesus. Even to be "born again" or to call yourself a Christian is no guarantee of true knowledge of God. The only true knowledge of God is to know God as *agape*, the sacrificial and self-giving love, the love revealed by Jesus on the cross. Only in this love and by this love may we truly know God.

This is the God we need, but it is not the God we want. The God we claim to seek is in fact the God from whom we would escape. Humanity is estranged from the true God because we are afraid of the demand of agape, the command to love God with all our heart and soul and strength and mind and to love our neighbour as ourselves. We are ashamed because we know we don't do it. Yet we also know that in this love is our true and only salvation, for ourselves individually, and for the whole human race.

All paths lead to God, or so it has been said. But they don't. People do seek God. Most people cry out to God at one time or another. Our reach and our seeking do not find God, but instead end up in the turmoil of our restless religiosity. The God we need

---

[87] T. S. Eliot, "Burnt Norton," pt. II, op. cit., p. 119.

is the One who comes to us, whose love is revealed in Jesus and
His cross.

I point beyond the gods of our human religiosity to the One
who is beyond our searching, our reasoning, our proofs, and our
words to the One who calls us to love one another but who
nevertheless accepts us as we are, idols and all. It is because we
see and know God's love in Christ that we can have faith and trust
in the grace and goodness of God.

Here, however, we run into trouble again, for our troubled
faith has largely lost the understanding of the meaning of faith.

CHAPTER 4

THE MEANING OF FAITH

Recapitulation

I have claimed that humanity is innately and incurably religious, needing some expression of our desire for God. But most human expressions of our need for God are idols, gods we create who will satisfy our wants. These gods—which can come in the form of money, power, happiness, self-fulfillment, family, nation, or systems of government—become our lords, our masters, and in the end we become slaves to our desires. The final idolatry is the worship of our own belief, our own religious expression, faith in our faith as distinct from faith in God.

We have looked at the Canaanite religion and their god, the Baal, as a prototype of such human idolatry—the god we call upon to provide for our security and prosperity. In contrast to the understanding of lordship that we find there, we have presented a different understanding of lordship in Jesus of Nazareth, the Christ, the image of God.

In the knowledge of the grace and love (*agape*), which we know in Jesus, we find the basis of our faith, our trust in the goodness and justice of God, and the ultimate righteousness of all creation. We now turn to an understanding of the meaning of faith.

Faith in What?

When my friend Greg was a teenager, he questioned things he had been taught or told, as teenagers do. He told his mother that he didn't believe in God. "Oh Greg," she said, "you must have faith!" To which he replied, "Faith in what?"

Greg is typical of many men and women of our time. In World War II, he was a navigator in the Royal Canadian Air Force. He told me of a bombing mission when it looked like they wouldn't make it back. He thought he was going to die, and he considered praying. But, he said, "I hadn't prayed in my life up until then, so I decided it wouldn't be honest to start at that point."

There is something admirable in the human courage of one who refuses to pray in the face of death, of Don Giovanni refusing to repent before the fires of hell. What is faith? Is it merely a means of escape in time of peril? A safeguard against eternal punishment for our sins?

Another friend, Lloyd, was out fishing in a small aluminium boat when the wind came up. He realized he was in trouble and he was about six miles offshore. He told me, "I couldn't pray for the storm to subside. I didn't have that kind of faith. I prayed for help that I might get home safely to my wife and daughters. A message came to me, to take one wave at a time. I did that. It took a long time for me to get home, but I made it." He believed that while he didn't have faith to command the wind to cease as Jesus did, the message which saved him came in some mysterious way as a result of the faith he did have and the prayer he uttered.

I recently watched a film documentary of interviews with people who had suffered heart problems. Each one had tried to bargain with God except for one man who said, "I knew the Lord was on my side and with His help, I might make it through. If not, I was in His hands." His faith was evident as he spoke.

Greg refused the possibility of faith. Lloyd, conscious that he couldn't get God to do what he wanted, nevertheless "knew the Lord was on his side and with God's help, he might make it through."

Christian faith today is a troubled faith in part because there is such general misunderstanding of the meaning of the word "faith," a misunderstanding that in large part has been fostered by the church itself. Faith, like love, is a short and seemingly simple word, but again like love it is one of the most misunderstood and misused words in the English language. In Paul Tillich's words,

> There is hardly a word in the religious language, both theological and popular, which is subject to more misunderstandings, distortions and questionable definitions than the word "faith." It

belongs to those terms which need healing before they can be
used for the healing of men. Today the term "faith" is more
productive of disease than of health. It confuses, misleads, creates
alternately skepticism and fanaticism, intellectual resistance and
emotional surrender, rejection of genuine religion and subjection
to substitutes. Indeed, one is tempted to suggest that the word
"faith" should be dropped completely; but desirable as that may
be it is hardly possible. A powerful tradition protects it. And there
is as yet no substitute expressing the reality to which the term
"faith" points. So, for the time being, the only way of dealing with
the problem is to try to reinterpret the word and remove the
confusing and distorting connotations, some of which are the
heritage of centuries.[88]

Many people look upon faith as an optional part of living, quite
unnecessary to life or happiness—likely a sign of old age or
psychological weakness. Others see faith as a kind of spiritual
willpower. Through faith, prayer, or devotion, we are able to get
from God what we want, whether getting out of a jam, healing our
diseases, or the salvation of our soul. Others understand faith as
believing what cannot be proved, accepting dogma, the teachings
of the church, whether or not they understand them or believe
them to be true.[89]

What is faith? Faith in what?

Faith is central to the Christian tradition. In the New Testament,
we read about "living by faith" and being "justified by faith." We
read in Hebrews that "faith is the substance of things hoped for, the
evidence of things not seen" (Hebrews 11:1), and in Ephesians, "by
grace you have been saved, through faith" (Ephesians 2:8), and also
that the Christian is instructed to "take the shield of faith"
(Ephesians 6:16). In reading the New Testament, it becomes clear
that faith is not, as many seem to think, a way of getting what we
want from God, whether health and healing, success in our
endeavours, or the salvation of our soul. Faith is trust in the grace
and goodness of God, the basis of a relationship with God. Faith is

---

[88] Paul Tillich, *Dynamics of Faith*, Harper Torchbooks, Harper & Brothers, New York,
1957, in his "Introductory Remarks."

[89] The word "dogma" originally comes from the Latin *docere*, to teach, and has come to
refer to the teachings of the church.

walking each day with a sense of God's presence and in the knowledge of God's love.

First Comes Faith

"Faith, hope and love abide, these three. But the greatest of these is Love" (I Corinthians 13:13). True, the greatest is love, but first comes faith.

We don't always recognize the importance of faith, even the necessity of faith, in our common living. Apart from religion, we don't think much about faith. But while we may consider religious faith to be optional, a kind of faith is nevertheless necessary in our everyday living. We have a certain amount of faith in the functioning of our social order—faith that the garbage will be picked up, that the restaurant won't serve us tainted food, faith that our doctor has the honest intention of healing us rather than killing us. We have a reasonable faith in the ordinary functioning of nature. While there are occasions when nature erupts with earthquake, flood, or hurricane, we can generally trust that the earth is not going to open at our feet and that the sun will rise and set on schedule.

Faith in what? Well, faith in others, or faith in the world around us. Such faith is necessary in our common living. Leo Tolstoy wrote,

> Wherever there is life, there is faith; since the origin of humankind faith has made it possible for us to live, and the main characteristics of faith are everywhere and always the same... Without faith, it is impossible to live.[90]

Pierre Duhem, a French physicist at the beginning of the twentieth century, was a devout Roman Catholic and because of this some claimed that he could not be a good scientist. In response, he wrote a long, impassioned apology claiming that without faith and trust in the order of creation and the constancy of the Creator, one could not be a scientist at all.

---

[90] Leo Tolstoy, *Confession,* IX

And faith comes first. It is not just that faith should come first but that faith *does* come first. "Faith precedes all attempts to derive it from something else, because these attempts are themselves based on faith."[91]

Faith comes before doubt. Before we doubt something, we must believe in something. Doubt is secondary.

As infants, we become aware of the reality around us. As we grow, we first accept the teachings passed on to us by our parents. Later we may question, but first we believe. We accept the worldview of our culture, the common understanding of the world and how things work. Later we may question, but first we believe. To quote Lesslie Newbigin,

> The primary part is opening one's mind to reality, opening one's mind to the tradition. One cannot begin to learn without faith, faith in the evidence of our senses, faith in the teaching of our parents, faith in the tradition that is embodied in the best books we study at school.... All of this is that foundation from which we begin to learn.[92]

Elsewhere he writes,

> The critical faculty is not self-sustaining. It can only develop on the basis of beliefs which are accepted—in the first instance, uncritically. If the capacity to believe is not developed along with the capacity to criticize, the result can only be fanaticism or nihilism.[93]

Our modern culture, the understanding of our existence that has developed over the past several hundred years, finds it difficult to grasp this truth. It is founded upon doubt, what has been called "the hermeneutics of suspicion." The early seventeenth century was a time, like our own, of upheaval and great confusion. It was

---

[91] Tillich, *Dynamics of Faith*, p. 8.

[92] Lesslie Newbigin, "What Is The Culture?" An unpublished address at the first regional conference of The Gospel and Our Culture Movement, held at High Leigh Conference Centre, Hoddesdon, Hertfordshire, England, October 15-17, 1990 and included in the conference booklet. Available from the British and Foreign Bible Society.

[93] Newbigin, *Learning for Living*, Vol. 17, No 2, Winter 1977, 'Teaching religion in a secular society,' p. 87.

in that time that the philosopher René Descartes, seeking certainty, decided to doubt everything he knew and imagined himself climbing into a stove. What would he know there in the darkness, deprived of all his senses? He concluded, "I think, therefore I am." (*Cogito ergo sum*.) This, he concluded, he knew for sure, and this was the starting point of his philosophical system.

So our scientific method of the last three hundred years, founded in large part on Descartes' philosophy, tests hypotheses by observing relevant data to discern what is true. It doubts. It questions. But before the question, before the test, there is the hypothesis, the data. In the words of Augustine, "Everyone who knows that he is in doubt about something knows a truth, and in regard to this thing that he knows he is certain... Consequently, whoever for whatever reason can doubt ought not to doubt that there is a truth."[94]

We will recognize the importance of doubt, and of asking questions, in order to understand. For the moment, recognize that "first comes faith." As Augustine claimed, faith is the foundation of knowledge. *Credo ut intelligam.* "I believe in order to understand." There is no understanding without first belief.

Before we begin to look at the particular understanding of faith in the New Testament, we need to remember how basic faith is to all our living. There are three great Christian "virtues"—faith, hope, and love. The greatest of these is love, but *first comes faith.*

Faith as Spiritual Willpower

Before we can begin to understand "faith" as the New Testament speaks of faith, we have to clear away the rust and the barnacles, the accretions of the years. It is regrettable, for it is so-called "people of faith" who have often caused misunderstanding, and yet it is necessary. When we have come to understand faith as the New

---

[94] In his sermon on Psalm 118 (Sermons xviii, 3) he says, "For although, unless he understands somewhat, no man can believe in God, nevertheless, by the very faith whereby he believes, he is helped to the understanding of greater things. For there are some things which we do not believe unless we understand them; and there are other things which we do not understand unless we believe them." Quoted by Niebuhr, *Human Nature*, p. 169.

Testament speaks of faith, we will see how very wrong, how bankrupt, are common understandings (or rather misunderstandings) of faith—for instance, faith as a kind of spiritual willpower.

As we have noted, many people see faith as a means of getting what they want from God. It may be fame and fortune, or it may be healing, or forgiveness of sins. It may be escape from the consequences of our actions, getting out of a jam we've gotten ourselves into, or it may be merely praying for our side to win the big game. A mother prays for her soldier son to be spared (a natural expression of her love). In time of war, both sides may be praying for God to be on their side, though as has been said, we should be more concerned whether we are on God's side.

All these have something in common—asking God to do something for us, maybe something trivial, maybe something significant. It is really a kind of spiritual willpower: if we only have faith, if we believe with all our might or pray with sufficient intensity, God will do what we ask. After all, doesn't the scripture say, "Ask and it will be given you" (Luke 11:29). We exhort one another to "have faith," and "only believe."

In fact, many Christians understand their salvation as being based on this kind of faith. "Saved by faith," is understood to mean that we are saved by believing certain things, and if they seem difficult to believe we should just try harder (I'll come back to this a bit later when we consider faith as assent).

Understanding faith as spiritual willpower results in the kind of idolatry we have been discussing, a god we want rather than the God we need. It seems common in all human religion—the desire to get a god, or gods, to serve us. From earliest times, people devised elaborate ceremonies and rituals to gain the favour of the gods or spirits of a certain place, often by sacrificing animals, and sometimes even their children. A temple in Japan we visited had a "prayer box" before the altar into which coins were dropped in the belief that "the god" might hear the money falling into the box and then come to hear the prayer. Think of the hundreds and hundreds of generations of humanity who have lived in fear of the divine, forming fearful images to represent a wrathful and capricious deity, seeking ways to appease or pacify the wrath of their "god."

Faith as spiritual will-power is not faith in the New Testament sense. Rather it is magic, whether practiced by some form of primitive animism or in the name of Jesus Christ. Magic is trying to get God to do what we want. Faith is opening our heart to what God wants, a relationship of love and trust. It is, of course, inevitable that we will be, at times, like little children calling to God and crying, "Notice me, I need you." We do need God and we will call on God in our need, whether the circumstances are trivial or life threatening.

This kind of faith doesn't have to be religious. It may have nothing to do with faith in God, and may be nothing more than superstition. Many people will believe, with Jiminy Cricket (in the Disney movie, *Pinocchio)*, "If you wish upon a star, your dreams come true." Consider the people, many of them quite intelligent, whose lives each day are guided to some degree by the astrology column in their daily newspaper. The myth of the happy ending is part of the American dream, the official optimism of our culture, the belief that, just when all seems lost, the cavalry will arrive with flags waving and trumpets blowing to save us.

This is not to deny the relationship we find in the Gospel between faith and healing. In Jesus' words, "Your faith has made you well" (for example, Mark 5:34). But in my experience, this healing faith is not a one-shot deal, called up on the spot, but a quality of life inherent in the person's attitude and way of living. In this regard, it seems to me that what we call "faith healing" is often possible.

I have known situations in my ministry where healing seemed unquestionably related to faith. I have prayed for healing and found healing happened, sometimes in extraordinary ways. I even seem to know when healing will happen and when it will not. No doubt "signs and wonders" should be more a part of ministry and Christian life than they have been.

But it should never be connected to hoopla, or working on people's emotions, and it should never be connected to money. A friend tells me of attending the healing service of a famous evangelist. The evangelist claimed that there were at least twenty people in the congregation at this particular service who could give $1,000 each to his ministry and called them to come forward. Twenty people did come forward. But then he refused to pray for them until they gave him the money. My friend left the service in disgust.

In any case, while God has promised perfect and permanent healing in the life to come, in this life, healing is partial and always impermanent. "Flesh and blood can not inherit the kingdom of God, nor does the perishable inherit the imperishable" (I Corinthians 15:50). Some have made the distinction between healings and cures. In this life, healing is impermanent and imperfect. For our complete and final cure, we must wait for our transformation into what the apostle Paul calls "spiritual bodies."

It is not in getting God to serve us, but in our service of God that we find our deepest happiness, fulfillment, and wholeness. It is as we live in the love of God (*agape*) and live that love in our relationship with others, loving even those who do not love us, that we find fulfillment. Faith, in the New Testament sense, is not getting what we want from God, but rather it is our response to God's grace in loving trust.

Faith as Assent

Another major misunderstanding of faith, and one that is especially barren of vitality and power, is faith as a kind of blind assent, "believing without evidence."[95]

There was a little boy who, when asked to define faith, replied, "Faith is how you believe what you don't think is true." Faith then becomes a means of believing what you're supposed to believe whether or not it appears to you to be true or to make sense. Faith is how you believe the things a Christian is supposed to believe, whether it is the doctrines and teaching of the church or those strange and miraculous occurrences recorded in the Bible that do not accord with our modern understanding of the workings of the world.

In the words of Thomas Aquinas, faith is "the act of the intellect assenting to a divine truth because of a movement of the will." The "angelic doctor," as he was called, went on to say that the will was empowered by the grace of God, but I would still consider it a downright dangerous definition. For faith can then become a kind of spiritual willpower—and the less sense a

---

[95] Note Paul Tillich, "The Intellectualistic Distortions of the Meaning of Faith," in *Dynamics of Faith*, pp. 30f.

statement makes, the more unbelievable, then all the more credit to you for believing it. It just shows that your faith is strong.[96]

In Lewis Carroll's *Though the Looking Glass*, the White Queen makes a preposterous statement, and Alice replies, "I can't believe that!" The Queen asks, "Can't you? Try again: draw a long breath, and shut your eyes."[97]So we go about exhorting each other to "have faith," and we admire those whose faith is so strong that it can withstand logic, evidence, or any kind of circumstance.

Again, this is a very different understanding of faith than that of the New Testament—faith as *assent* to a truth rather than trust in God's grace. The Latin word is *assensus,* and it refers to belief in a proposition or doctrine. It is an intellectual thing, head rather than heart.

It is important, of course, to have an intellectual understanding of our faith, a reason for our beliefs, but there is no doubt that the personal element of trust is primary in the New Testament. The content of our faith, what we believe, is important, but surely the context of our faith (the relationship with God out of which faith springs) is primary.

The dispute between these two elements runs down through the history of Christian thought. The Latin root of our word "faith," *fides,* has intimations of both assent and trust. There has been a continuing debate between those who emphasize the "objective factors" of faith, and those who emphasize the "subjective factors" of faith—between faith as "that which one believes" (*fides qua creditur*) and faith as "that by which one believes" (*fides quae creditur*).

Consider our use of the word "knowledge." Faith and knowledge are, I most earnestly believe, not opposites, but closely allied. There are two words for knowledge in French, compared to the single one in English. There is *savoir,* for knowing some "thing," knowledge of or about something or someone. They say *connaître* for direct and personal knowledge, knowing someone rather than knowing about someone.

---

[96] Tillich, *Dynamics of Faith,* "The Voluntaristic Distortions of the Meaning of Faith," pp. 35f.

[97] Lewis Carroll, *Alice's Adventures in Wonderland & Though the Looking Glass,* A Signet Classic, published by The New American Library, New York, 1960, chp. 5, p. 174.

For the Greeks, knowledge was more apt to mean scientific or philosophical knowledge, knowledge about things. For the Hebrews, it was more important to have personal, relational knowledge. In Hebrew understanding, one of the deepest and truest forms of knowledge existed in the marriage relationship: "And Abram *knew* Sarah, and she conceived...." In biblical understanding, personal knowledge is more important than objective knowledge. Sadly, we have too largely lost this more essential element of understanding—faith as a loving trust in the One whom Jesus called *Abba.*[98]

I find it tragic that faith is so largely understood as assent. Think of the history of the church, down through the centuries. Again and again we see the persecution, the torture, even the burning at the stake of those called "heretics" because they would not "assent" to official doctrines of the church, and "chose" instead to hold contrary beliefs (The root of the word "heresy" is the Greek *haeresis*, meaning a choice. A heretic is one who chooses a belief rather than simply believing what is taught).

The great peril of orthodoxy, understood as true and correct belief as defined by the church, is that it is often a matter of legislation rather than an ideal. In one way of looking at it, the Emperor Constantine, when he established Christianity as the one religion of the Roman Empire in the early years of the fourth century, did the church very serious harm. He allowed the bishops of the church of the time to define true and correct doctrine. He didn't tell the theologians what to believe, but he did insist that they had to come up with one agreed upon understanding that all would have to accept. It may be that Constantine believed that a unified Christendom was needed to hold together his tottering empire.

The great Church Councils of the fourth century laboured to come to one acceptable statement of Christian doctrine. After lengthy and heated debate, over several decades, they came up with the statement of faith called "the Nicene Creed." This, with

---

[98] *Abba* is the name commonly used by Jesus of God. It was the name used in family life of the father of the family, intimating both familiarity and trust. Its continued use in the early church is indicated at two places in the New Testament, Romans 8:15 and Galatians 4:6.

the Apostles' Creed and the Athanasian Creed, became the authorized statements of Christian orthodoxy and unity.[99]

The Athanasian Creed, especially, is a lengthy and complex statement of doctrine, difficult even for trained theologians to understand:

> We worship one God in Trinity, and the Trinity in Unity; neither confusing the Persons, nor dividing the substance.
> For there is one Person of the Father, another of the Son, another of the Holy Ghost;
> But the Godhead of the Father and of the Son and of the Holy Ghost is all one, the glory equal, the majesty co-eternal.
> Such as the Father is, such is the Son, and such is the Holy Ghost;
>   . . .
> The Father eternal, the Son eternal, the Holy Ghost eternal;
> And yet there are not three eternals, but one eternal!
> The Father is made of none, nor created, nor begotten.
> The Son is of the Father alone; not made, nor created, but begotten.
> The Holy Ghost is of the Father and the Son; not made, nor created, nor begotten, but proceeding.

And it ends with this statement:

> This is the Catholic Faith, which except a man (sic) do faithfully and steadfastly believe, he cannot be saved.

Martin Luther did much to help the church to understand again the element of faith as trust. It was when he read the verse, "The just shall live by faith" (Romans 1:17), and understood that it meant trust in God's grace, that he wrote, "I felt myself to be reborn and to have gone through the open doors into paradise."[100]

But Protestantism soon developed its own orthodox faith. It lacked the formal authority of the Roman church, but it did command a strong element of spiritual coercion. Protestantism, too, has had its heresy trials, and yes, its burnings—all in the name of "the Prince of peace."

---

[99] Note "Creeds of Christendom," in *An Encyclopedia of Religion*, ed. Vergilius Ferm, The Philosophical Library, New York, 1945, pp. 207-208.

[100] Quoted in Roland H. Bainton, *Here I Stand: A Life of Martin Luther*, Published by New American Library for Abingdon Press, Nashville, 4th printing, 1987, p. 49.

Far from finding any merit in faith of this sort, I find it a source of dismay.

First, is it not basically dishonest and hypocritical to suggest that you can believe something that you really don't think is true? Surely honest agnosticism is preferable to hypocritical belief.

Second, this kind of faith bespeaks an authoritarianism that treats people as less than human, less than autonomous and free. In this sense, the heretic is more human than the blind believer, for by his very name he has asserted his freedom and declared his right to choose.

Third, this understanding of faith is not Biblical. It makes faith a result of our own efforts rather than the gift of God. It makes faith into a new kind of spiritual achievement by which we "win" our salvation—the very thing that Paul (and Luther) fought against with so much vehemence. Faith, they said, is possible for us because of God's grace, shown to us in Jesus Christ. Because we see in Christ the Love of God for us, therefore we know we can trust God—have faith in God. To turn again and say that faith is something that we *must* have in order to be acceptable to God is to fall into the old trap again—to make faith into a new kind of "works," something that we can or must do to be acceptable to God.

And fourth, such an understanding easily results in self-righteousness. If faith is the result of my own willpower, then it may become a cause for pride. If I stand up and recite the Apostles' Creed, or say the prayers and sing the hymns with a good, strong voice, then I may look upon myself as one of the righteous ones, whether or not there is any love in my heart and grace in my living.[101]

The cross is the central symbol of our faith. When I stand before the cross, when I think of the stupendous claims made for Jesus of Nazareth, I realize that I, too, am a doubter, a heretic. I find I must question and seek to understand. There is much about this man, Jesus, His life and death and resurrection, that I don't understand; so many things in the Bible and in Christian doctrine which I find difficult. There are some things I can't accept just by closing my eyes and

---

[101] Of course, the recitation of the creed in public worship can be a very meaningful expression of our faith if done "in spirit and in truth."

taking a deep breath. What makes it valid for me is not my belief, my opinions or convictions, but God's love in Christ. "God so loved the world" (John 3:16). And that means me, too.

That's what this cross is all about. I am not right in every detail of belief, as I am not righteous in all my dealings and doings. And so the cross becomes the basis of my faith, my trust. I cherish the words of Quaker poet John Greenleaf Whittier:

> O friends, with whom my feet have trod
> The quiet aisles of prayer,
> Good witness of your zeal for God
> And love of man I bear.
>
> I trace your lines of argument,
> Your logic linked and strong.
> I weigh as one who dreads dissent,
> And fears a doubt as wrong.
>
> But still my human hands are weak
> To hold your iron creeds:
> Against the words ye bid me speak
> My heart within me pleads.
>
> Who fathoms the Eternal Thought?
> Who talks of scheme and plan?
> The Lord is God! He needeth not
> The poor device of man!
>
> I see the wrong that round me lies,
> I feel the guilt within;
> I hear, with groan and travail-cries,
> The world confess its sin.
>
> Yet in the maddening maze of things,
> And tossed by storm and flood,
> To one fixed trust my sprit clings:
> I know that God is good!
>
> I know not where His islands lift
> Their fronded palms in air;
> I only know I cannot drift
> Beyond His love and care.[102]

---

[102] From "The Eternal Goodness," *The Poetical Works of John Greenleaf Whittier,* ed. William Michael Rossetti, Ward, Lock & co. Limited, London, New York and Melbourne, (no date), pp. 397-398.

Faith as Trust

Therefore, since we are justified by faith, we have peace with God through our Lord Jesus Christ. Through Him we have obtained access to this grace in which we stand, and we rejoice in our hope of sharing the glory of God... God shows His love for us in that while we were yet sinners, Christ died for us (Romans 5:1-2, 8).

The point of all our living and our believing is love—the love of God we can know in Jesus Christ. In this self-giving, sacrificial love, we find the highest expression of our humanity, the fulfillment we seek, the very spirit of life in the kingdom of God. But, as we claimed, before love comes faith—faith not as spiritual willpower or intellectual assent, but a trust in God's grace basic to all our living. Faith, in this sense, means walking each day with a sense of God's presence and in the knowledge and confidence of God's love. Martin Luther wrote,

This it is to behold God in faith—that you should look upon His fatherly, friendly heart, in which there is not anger nor ungraciousness. For faith leads you in and opens up God's heart and will, that you should see pure grace and overflowing love."[103]

This is what the New Testament means by "faith." While there are many nuances to the way different Biblical writers speak of faith, it is possible to speak of a core understanding:

… the meaning goes back to a Hebrew concept which was brought to full actuality in the relation with God established for Christians in Christ. The core of this Hebrew concept is firmness, reliability, or steadfastness. To believe is to hold on to something firmly, with conviction and confidence. It is implied that steadfastness is sought in the object believed, and that in laying hold of the object, the believer himself will become steadfast.... Usually it is a person, rather than a statement, which is believed; and in the context of men's relations to God the verb always

---

[103] Bainton, op. cit., p. 50.

implies personal conviction and trust arising with direct personal relationship.[104]

To "live by faith," in the New Testament sense, is to trust that at the very centre of life there beats the heart of the One whom Jesus called *Abba* (meaning a loving father). To "live by faith" is to live with a sense of the presence of that loving, caring Spirit and in the knowledge of God's love. From such faith issues the fruits of the Spirit of God—love, joy, hope, and peace.

FAITH IS PERSONAL

If we understand faith first of all as trust, trust in the love and the goodness of God, then we must understand faith as personal and relational. It is to say that God is Person, and our relation with God can be a personal relationship, an "I-Thou" relationship.[105]

Faith, as the New Testament speaks of it, is not first of all belief in a statement, but trust in a friend—not an intellectual opinion, but a way of life. It is not so much acceptance of doctrine, dogma, or creed, but trust in the grace and goodness of God known to us in Jesus, whom we call Christ. It is the confidence that life is finally good, that chaos and death are not triumphant in the end, and that at the centre of our existence there beats the heart of a loving Father.

God is Person—not Philosophical Premise or Mechanical Power. Not a person, but *the* Person, of whom our personhood is but a dim reflection. And in Jesus we know that God is gracious, not standing back in judgment, but reaching out in love to each one of us, whatever our condition or our history. And because God is Person and God is gracious, we can respond to God's searching love, entering into a relationship with God "through faith."

In the fullest sense, faith is a living relationship with the One whom Jesus called *Abba*. It is the confidence that, even in the worst that life can bring, we are loved and held and cherished.

Faith is our part of the relationship. For us, it means being faithful, being responsible to the relationship.

---

[104] W. A. Whitehouse, in *A theological Wordbook of the Bible*, Ed. Alan Richardson, The Macmillan Company, New York, 1953, p. 75.

[105] Re philosopher Martin Buber's *I and Thou*, first published in 1923. Buber distinguished personal relationship ("I-Thou") from objective relationships ("I-It").

If someone tells us something, we may believe it because it seems to be true, or because we trust the person who tells it to us. As Paul writes, "I know whom I have believed, and am convinced that He is able to keep that which I've committed to Him" (II Timothy 1:12). But we don't trust people unless we know them, have been together, worked together, and talked together. When we have developed that kind of a relationship, there is trust.

Faith is relational and personal. It doesn't come wrapped in fancy paper and fine ribbons like a present on one's birthday when all we have to do is break the ribbon and tear off the paper. It's not like buying a new car, shopping around until you decide what model you want, then going in and making a deal, putting the money down, and driving away.

It's more like friendship, a relationship without conditions that grows through the years. "I have called you friends," Jesus said to His disciples (John 15:15), speaking about a relationship of equality and freedom. Many a person who has walked by faith in Christ over the years can tell you what that friendship has meant. "He walks with me and He talks with me, and He tells me I am His own"[106]—one of the beloved hymns in an earlier day when life was uncertain and often very, very lonely. This is more than just sentiment; it speaks of a relationship deep, precious, and transformational.

As it is personal and relational, faith is not mechanical. Some prayer groups seem to be wired in such a way that, when one prayer sits down another jumps to his feet as though part of an electric circuit. Nor is it mere emotion, a result of repeated praise choruses and emotion-stirring preaching. God's presence is not realized by some sort of mechanical or electrical connection, nor by artificial stimulation of the emotions.

How then do we know God's presence? If we say, it is by faith—what does that mean? It is not a knowledge that comes through the five "senses" (from the Latin *sensus*, meaning literally "the faculty of perceiving"). It is not just seeing, but seeing through the reality that our senses present to us, as when we look

---

[106] From the old Gospel hymn "In the garden," by C. Austin Miles, copyright 1912 by Hall-Mack Co.

at a sunset and, aware of something more than the colours, we sense the mystery of beauty. We look at a painting and perceive a deeper reality. We listen to good music, well presented, whether it is Bach or the Blues, and we become aware of something more than the music. We become aware of the wonder and glory and beauty of life, in spite of its ambiguities. We are lifted out of ourselves and become aware of something transcendent. We are sitting with someone we love, not touching, not looking, but simply aware of his or her presence.

Perhaps we can speak of our awareness of God as a pre-sense, an awareness that precedes or transcends consciousness. "Faith does not mean believing without evidence. It means believing in realities that go beyond sense and sight—for which a totally different sort of evidence is required."[107]

While some come to faith with a dynamic conversion experience, for most of us faith has a quiet beginning. It then grows through the years, often imperceptibly from day to day and week to week, through all the ups and downs of life, surviving the potholes, the mistakes we make, and the cuts and hurts and broken bones that just seem to happen.

We can't create faith, or command it. It is the gift of God. But we can receive it, and nurture it. If we don't, it withers and dies.

Some of us enjoy gardening—digging in the earth and cultivating, planting and watering, fertilizing and weeding. We give our gardens every possible care. Faith is rather like that. Nothing we can do will make a seed come to life and grow. Only God can accomplish that, but if we don't tend that seed which God's Word has planted in our hearts, if we don't care for it and nurture it, it's not going to amount to much. If we let the weeds get ahead of us, or if we neglect to nourish and water regularly, then the plant which is our faith will wither and perhaps die. When we need it and turn to it, as we all do sooner or later, we find that there is nothing there.

---

[107] John Baillie, in *Draper's book of Quotations for the Christian World*, Edythe Draper, Tyndale House Publishers, Inc., Wheaton, Ill., 1992, Item #3672.

OUR NEED OF FAITH IN TESTING TIMES

There are times in our lives when we become very conscious of our need of faith. Every life needs an altar and faith for testing times. It's important that we be prepared for these times.

In summer, when the weather is warm and the nights are mild, it's relatively simple to get along without some sort of protecting shelter. But in the winter, it's important to have a roof over our heads and four solid walls around us to protect us from the elements. Even so, during the summery periods of our lives, when we are young and strong and troubles and worries are relatively few, faith may not seem important. But when we are overtaken by life's difficulties and uncertainties, by suffering and despair and death, then we earnestly and urgently desire the strength and confidence which faith alone can give.

The tragedy, of course, is that while most of us realize the necessity of being prepared for winter, we neglect to build our house of faith until the cold winds of life begin to blow and the desolating storms of life's bitterest experiences begin to sweep around us. Then we begin to cry, pitifully, some almost-forgotten verse of scripture taught to us as a child, or to mutter the Lord's Prayer as though it were some sort of magic spell—like a man trying to knock a couple of old boards together in the middle of a howling blizzard because he neglected to build himself a shelter when the weather was fine and warm.

Sooner or later in life, for almost any person, faith, our relationship with God, our trust in the goodness of God, will become important to us, more important than anything else in our lives.

One time when I was at the local hospital visiting members of my congregation, a nurse came running up to me. "Mr. Reynolds, can you come? A child has been killed in an accident." We walked down a hall, turned the corner on a long corridor. I could see a small group at the other end. Then I heard a woman cry out, almost a scream, "Oh thank God, it's Mr. Reynolds!" She was not of my congregation. I didn't know her. That didn't matter. It wasn't me in particular that she wanted. Her child had been killed and at that moment the most important thing to her was someone who could speak a word of faith.

Ministers see a lot of tragedy in their work, but sometimes the tragedies that give the greatest sorrow are when people think they have faith, perhaps once did have faith, but have neglected it, have let it wither and die. Perhaps they had a "Sunday School faith" that was never tested, and so they never developed a mature faith. Perhaps it was a "second hand faith" that they never made their own. When the testing time came, what they thought was there was gone and they were left doubly bereft.

If you are young and have never run into one of these experiences that really test your mettle, please, please, don't allow yourself to be unaware of them or unprepared for them. They will come. And you'll need courage, strength, and endurance. But most of all, you'll need faith. You'll need it desperately. But if you wait until then, you won't know where to turn, and you won't know how to find it. If you once had faith, but tucked it away in a corner of your life and neglected it, you'll find that it has seeped away, and where it once was, there is now only an empty space.

Even then, of course, you may still turn to God and know that God is there for you. In such a time, you may turn away from God in bitterness and anger, or you may turn to God in your bitterness and anger and seek comfort and strength in God's presence and grace.

FAITH IS LIFE-GIVING, NOT LIFE-DENYING

But it's not just a matter of walking with God in the sunshine so that God will walk with you in the storm. The occasional times in our lives when we are desperately aware of our need of faith simply point us to a need that is constantly there. To walk by faith is to live in a whole new dimension of joy and peace.

For this living and walking with a sense of God's gracious presence is not a grim and onerous burden we assume against the day of disaster. Faith, in this sense, not only makes the bad times better, but it also makes the good times better still.

Too long has Christian faith been regarded as negative, life-denying. "Thou hast conquered, O pale Galilean, and the world has grown grey from Thy breath."[108] Rather Jesus said, "I came that they may have *life*, and have it abundantly" (John 10:10).

---

[108] Algernon Swinburne, "Hymn to Proserpine," The Oxford Dictionary of Quotations, Third Edition, Oxford University Press, Oxford, New York, Toronto, Melbourne, 1979, p. 530.

Faith means holding and developing that attitude toward life and relationship with God and with one another that fills out the dimensions of our own lives and gives us a fuller measure of living, the full flavour of this sweet-and-sour experience we call life. Living by faith, as the New Testament speaks of it, results in increasing love, joy, and peace; the fruits of life lived in free and grateful relationship with God. Faith is not a denial of the fullness of life. Quite the opposite. It is positive, not negative.

If our religious faith is not giving freedom and wholeness, then there is something wrong with our religious faith. Faith is not just something we need in testing times. It must give an additional flavour to our lives in the ordinary course of our living and in our happiest moments.

FAITH THAT ENDURES

This kind of faith endures, in spite of trial.

> It is habitual with us to imagine salvation as something either momentary or occasional—a special intervention in which God makes sure of the eternal disposition of our souls. But it is total. It is comprehensive. It is world embracing, history girdling, life penetrating.[109]

It is the faith of Abraham who trusted God to do what God promised, to make of him a great nation even though at ninety-nine years of age he was still childless. It is the faith of Job who trusted God in spite of the tragedies in his own life.

It was the faith of the African American people brought as slaves to this continent, treated not as human beings but as property. In one state, you could be hanged for stealing a chicken, but your slave was your property and you could beat, rape, mutilate, and even murder them with legal impunity. Faith didn't relieve their oppression, but it did give them comfort and strength to endure the here and now in the hope of rest and peace to come in the promises of God.

---

[109] Eugene H. Peterson, *Answering God: The Psalms as Tools for Prayer*, Harper San Francisco, first HarperCollins paperback edition, 1991, p. 114.

Composer Gavin Bryars' "Jesus' Blood Never Failed Me Yet" features an elderly voice singing an old Gospel song with orchestral accompaniment. Here is the story behind the piece as he tells it.

> In 1971, when I lived in London, I was working on a film about people living rough in the area round Elephant and Castle and Waterloo Station. In the course of being filmed, some people broke into drunken song—sometimes bits of opera, sometimes sentimental ballads—and one, who in fact did not drink, sang a religious song, "Jesus' Blood Never Failed Me Yet." This was ultimately not used in the film and I was given all the unused sections of tape, including this one.
>
> When I played it at home, I found that his singing was in tune with my piano, and I improvised a simple accompaniment. I noticed, too, that the first section of the song—13 bars in length— formed an effective loop which repeated in a slightly unpredictable way. I took the tape loop to Leicester, where I was working in the Fine Art Department, and copied the loop onto a continuous reel of tape, thinking about adding an orchestrated accompaniment. The door of the recording room opened on to one of the large painting studios and I left the tape copying, with the door open, while I went to have a cup of coffee. When I came back I found the normally lively room unnaturally subdued. People were moving about much more slowly than usual and a few were sitting alone, quietly weeping.
>
> I was puzzled until I realized that the tape was still playing and that they had been overcome by the old man's singing. This convinced me of the emotional power of the music and the possibilities offered by adding a simple, though gradually evolving, orchestral accompaniment that respected the tramp's nobility and simple faith.[110]

Here was a person in the meanest condition singing, "This I know, for He loves me so. Jesus' blood never failed me yet." You could take the attitude that his faith didn't do him much good, or you might stop and wonder what it had meant to him over the years with whatever life had brought along. He sang it over and over, clinging to those words, that message which seemed to give him comfort and strength to carry on.

---

[110] from Gavin Bryars' Official Web Site, www.gavinbryars.com, discography, June 8, 2005.

In the Hebrew scriptures, the word for "hope" and the word for "wait" come from a common root, the verb meaning "to stretch." It is when our faith is stretched by hoping and waiting that it may become strong.

SPIRITUAL CAPITAL

We use the word "capital" for accumulated wealth, which may also be passed on from one generation to the next. I have come to believe that there is also spiritual capital, the fruit of a life of faith that may also be passed from one generation to the next.

There are many good and fine people I know who show no evidence in their lives of anything we might call faith. But I am more and more impressed as I grow older that there seems to be something in the lives of these good but faithless people that seems to run out over the generations.

Conversely, where parents or grandparents have been people of deep faith, there often seems to be a kind of "spiritual capital" that often carries over to children and grandchildren.

My first pastoral charge as a young minister was in a rural area of southern New Brunswick that had been settled by Irish Protestants at the time of one of the potato famines in Ireland. The church records went back over one hundred years to those earlier times.

Studying those records, I became aware that there seemed to be a rough correlation between the character of individuals who lived back then and the character of their children and grand-children living there in my time, more than one hundred years later. Those old church records indicated, by the activity and participation of that ancestor in the life of the church then, the kind of person the ancestor was. And eight or nine times out of ten, that indicated the kind of person their descendant might be—because that person, living one hundred years later, the grandchild or great-grandchild of those early settlers, was so often like the ancestor in character and quality of personality. Always remember, the kind of person you are, and the quality of your own faith, may influence the kind of person your children and grandchildren will be, even to three and four generations.

First Comes Faith

Faith, hope, and love. The point of it all is love, that self-giving, self-sacrificing spirit which we see in Jesus' life, ministry, and death. But first comes faith, life lived in humble and grateful relationship with God, in loving trust in God's grace. The result is an increase in our lives of that quality which we see in Jesus' life and ministry and supremely in the cross—*agape* love. We may see it in our increasing love for others, not only for those we love the most, but also for those who are difficult to love, even our enemies. Love is the fruit, but first comes faith.

CHAPTER 5

CAN GOD BE GOOD?

The Problem

We have looked at faith as necessary for all our living, as the foundation of all our knowledge. We have thought about the mis-understanding of faith that sees it as a kind of magic, a spiritual willpower that gets God to do what we want. We distinguished between faith as "assent" (to a doctrine or dogma) and faith as "trust" (in the grace and faithfulness of God known to us in Jesus Christ). But, without a doubt, there have been a few keen types who have wanted to say, "Yes, but you just keep assuming that the Christian faith is true, that God is good and is worthy of our trust. But when I look at life, I see a lot of things that make it very difficult to believe that God is good."

Many find it difficult to believe in the goodness of God in the face of nature "red in tooth and claw" and the terrible suffering of children and innocent people, not always caused by the inhumanity of humanity but often by what have been called "acts of God." This, to my mind and faith, is the central problem of Christian faith.

The traditional statement of faith of the both Protestant and Catholic churches is called "The Apostles' Creed."[111] The most

---

[111] "I believe in God, the Father almighty, creator of heaven and earth. I believed in Jesus Christ, his only Son, our Lord. He was conceived by the power of the Holy Spirit, and born of the virgin Mary. He suffered under Pontius Pilate, was crucified , dead, and buried. He descended to the dead. On the third day he rose again. He ascended into heaven, and is seated at the right hand of the Father. He will come again to judge the living and the dead. I believe in the Holy Spirit, the holy Catholic Church, the communion of saints, the forgiveness of sins, the resurrection of the body and the life everlasting. Amen." *(The Book of Alternative Services of the Anglican Church of Canada, Anglican Book Center, Toronto, Canada, 1985, p. 52.)*

difficult part of the Apostles' Creed for me is not the bit about "conceived by the Holy Ghost," nor "He descended to the dead," nor the part about the "resurrection of the body." Those are the parts that seem to cause people the most difficulty. I think I've come to some understanding of what they mean—or at least what they mean to me.

No, the part that bothers me most, the part I find most difficult to accept, is the very first phrase where it says, "I believe in God the Father Almighty."

How, in the face of the evil and suffering of the world, is it possible to say that God is both like a father and also almighty? Must we not rather say that God may be like a loving parent, unwilling to see us suffer, but lacking almightiness, unable to do anything about it—He would if He could, but He can't. Or on the other hand, we may say that God is almighty but not "like a father," able to do something about it but not willing to do anything—He could if He would, but He won't.

Go to the street corner where the little girl, coming home from school, was struck and killed by a drunken driver. Visit the pioneer cemetery and read on the tombstones the mute testimony that half the community was wiped out in one winter through some disease, probably diphtheria or pneumonia. December 26, 2005, Boxing Day, the day after Christmas, an undersea earthquake in the Indian Ocean caused a massive tidal wave, a tsunami, with waves up to fifteen meters. Some 200,000 people were killed and large areas of South Asia were devastated. It is reasonable for people to ask, "Can God be good?"

Walk into the cancer ward of one of our hospitals for sick children where you'll see three- and four-year-old children fighting the terrible and sometimes hopeless battle against cancer, often facing great pain and the fearsome consequences of desperate treatments. Stand there and then say, "I believe in God, the Father Almighty."

Of course, this is only a problem to the person who desires to believe in a God who is both good and all-powerful. It's not the same problem for the person who denies the existence of God or the goodness of God. The problem for them is even more difficult—how to explain the measure of meaning and goodness and love which we *do* experience.

But for the person who seeks to believe that God is good and almighty, and who knows that pain and evil are very real and very terrible, there is a conflict here that defies human understanding. In the face of human suffering, perhaps in the midst of our own pain, we cry, "If God is good, surely it is not God's will that we should suffer so. But if God is God, He must be willing for suffering to happen."

> I heard upon his dry dung heap
> That man cry out who cannot sleep:
> "If God is God, He is not good,
> If God is good, He is not God."[112]

We'll come back to face the problem, but before we go further, let us think of the alternatives. One alternative is gods who are not good. Through human history people have believed in God or gods. Commonly they have been gods of ugly visage, capricious, or malicious, whose wrath had to be somehow appeased, usually by ritual or some form of sacrifice, lest their deviousness control our lives. Today, however, there seems to be another alternative—not evil gods, but no gods. As twentieth century poet T. S. Eliot noted,

> It seems something has happened that has never happened before: though we know not just when, or why, or how, or where.
>
> Men have left God not for other gods, they say, but for no god; and this has never happened before.[113]

I want to suggest to you that *if you look at all the evidence, you'll find it's easier to believe than it is to disbelieve.* Yes, life is ambiguous. It's not simple. As Einstein said, "The Lord God is subtle." But remember that he added, "But God is never mali-

---

[112] from *J.B.*, by Archibald MacLeish, The Riverside Press, Cambridge, MA, 1956, p.m14, The Prologue.
[113] T. S. Eliot, *Choruses from "The Rock,"* VII, *The Complete Poems and Plays, 1909-1950*, Harcourt, Brace and World, Inc., New York, 1952, p. 108.

cious."[114] Life may be ambiguous, but in balance and considering all the evidence, I suggest it is easier to believe than it is to believe in nothing.

Have You Tried Doubting Your Doubts?

If you feel bothered by doubt, I invite you to go ahead and examine your beliefs. Question the things you have been taught. But don't stop there. Keep on. Doubt your doubts. Question them as thoroughly as you have questioned your faith. I think you will find that, while many things you think you should believe may fall, in the end you will find that belief makes more sense than unbelief.

Too many times, I have had someone, usually someone young, tell me that they went to a priest or a pastor with questions about their faith, only to be told that they should not question, only believe. Of course, if faith is "assent," intellectual assent to the teaching of the church, then doubt is wrong.

If faith is "trust," then doubt may not be such a bad thing after all. It is, in fact, the only way that false beliefs can be shown to be false, that bad customs may be replaced by good customs, that ancient idols may be toppled from their thrones. We can understand Aristotle saying that "doubt is the beginning of belief," and Galileo calling doubt "the father of discovery."

People once believed that the earth was flat. But Christopher Columbus said, "I can't believe that!" and sailed on until he discovered the Americas.

Martin Luther was taught to accept the penitential system of the medieval church and the sale of indulgences as a means of salvation. He said, "I can't believe that!" He tacked his "protest" to the door of the parish church of Wittenberg, and the Protestant Reformation was begun.

When the steam engine was new, there was speculation that perhaps ships might be equipped with it and even run the whole course of the Atlantic Ocean powered completely by steam. Someone wrote a book showing the impracticability of it, but one

---

[114] Inscription above the fireplace in Fine Hall, Princeton University, from a remark made at Princeton during the week of May 9, 1921. *The Oxford Dictionary of Modern Quotations, ed. Tony Augarde, Oxford University Press, Oxford, New York, 1991, p. 72.*

person who read that book exclaimed, "I don't believe it." Indeed, the first boat to cross the Atlantic solely by steam carried a copy of that same book.[115]

Jesus of Nazareth, in this sense, was one of the greatest of doubters. The Jewish people considered the Samaritans to be an ignoble and inferior people with whom proper Jews should have no dealings. Jesus refused to judge all the people of Samaria by that notion, and told the story of a good Samaritan who was a better person than either the priest or the lawyer.

He was taught that pleasing God meant keeping every letter of the Law. "I don't believe it!" He said, and taught that healing the sick was more important than keeping laws of the Sabbath, and that justice and mercy were more important than tithing herbs.

Progress, the development of truth, is built upon such doubters—the questioners who stop to think and to inquire.

Moreover, isn't doubt necessary to real faith? We don't attain real faith through *ostrichism,* sticking our head in the sand in order to believe. Real faith is not hereditary. It's not something we're born with, something we inherit from our parents. We must find it for ourselves. A creed is the expression of someone else's faith, not ours. It is something outside ourselves. It is not ours until we test it, question it, doubt it, and wrestle with it as Jacob wrestled with the stranger in the pre-dawn darkness (Genesis 32:22f.)

Only by facing our doubts, looking them dead in the eye, will we come to a faith that is ours, that is strong and secure. Then we may come to understand, believe, and cherish it for ourselves. We can't claim faith for our own unless we have faced the possibility that there is "nothing there," until we have taken the risk, like Peter, of stepping out of the boat onto the water (Matthew 14:28f.)

Read Alfred Lord Tennyson's poem in memory of his friend Arthur Hallam. Feel in it the very real struggle that goes on between belief and unbelief. Read the tribute to the friend who,

... fought his doubts and gathered strength,
He would not make his judgments blind,
He faced the spectres of the mind

---

[115] Note Harry Emerson Fosdick, "The Importance of Doubting our Doubts," in *Great Preaching Today*, ed. Alton M. Motter, Harper & Brothers, New York, 1955, pp.52f.

And laid them, thus he came at length
To find a stronger faith his own.

And so Tennyson wrote,

There is more faith in honest doubt,
Believe me, than in half the creeds.[116]

Harry Emerson Fosdick, a famous preacher of the twentieth century, was brought up in strict fundamentalism. His grandmother told him that if he did not believe that Jonah was swallowed by a whale, he should in good logic abandon the Bible and all religion. He tells of his struggle.

When I started for college in my junior year, I told my mother that I was going to clear God out of the universe and begin all over to see what I could find. I could not swallow the Christian faith unquestioningly. I had to fight for it. And so it's mine. Every doubt raised against it, every question asked about it, I have faced often with agony of mind. I am not afraid of them.

But by disbelieving in God I did not escape belief: I ran headlong into belief in aetheism, materialism, into faith that the ultimate, creative factors in the universe are physical particles operating blindly without mind behind them or purpose in them. Talk about credulity! ...

And now in my elder years, what a Christian of the last generation said, I understand, "Who never doubted, never half believed!"[117]

It's hard, sometimes, to believe. But it's harder, much harder it seems to me, not to believe in anything.

And now what are we? Unbelievers both,
Calm and complete, determinately fixed
Today, tomorrow, and forever pray?
You'll grant me that? Not so, I think!
In no wise! All we've gained is that belief,
Like unbelief before, shakes us by fits,

---

[116] "In Memoriam," XCV, in *Poems of Tennyson*, Henry Frowde, Oxford University Press, London, New York and Toronto, 1908, p. 416.
[117] Fosdick, *Dear Mr. Brown: Letters to a Person Perplexed about Religion*, Harper & Row, Publishers, New York and Evanston, 1961, p. 21, and "The Importance of Doubting our Doubts," p. 95.

Confounds us like its predecessor. Where's
The gain? How can we guard our unbelief,
Make it bear fruit to us?—The problem here.
Just when we are safest, there's a sunset touch,
A fancy from a flower-bell, someone's death,
A chorus ending from Euripides –
And that's enough for fifty hopes and fears
As old and new at once as nature's self,
To rap and knock and enter in our soul,
Take hands and dance there.[118]

Do you think that you can settle comfortably into disbelief? Just when all seems settled, there comes the glory of a sunset, the mystery a microscope reveals, the birth of your baby, the death of a friend, the wonder of someone who loves you—and our *un*belief is shaken to the core.

Realize this. The real antithesis of faith, its real opposite, is not doubt, but *fear*. If faith is trust, its opposite is lack of trust—fear, anxiety. This is what "doubt" originally meant in the New Testament—that existential anxiety which comes from lack of trust in the rightness of things, lack of confidence in the ultimate victory of righteousness.

It is *fear* of which we need to be afraid. Fear is the enemy of our age, attacking our will, our heart, our intellect, and making us an impotent culture, unable to come to terms with our problems, in spite of our power and all our wealth. It is fear that seems to drive us to our own destruction in spite of ourselves. We're afraid to feed the hungry lest we might have to sacrifice something ourselves. We're afraid to deal with environmental problems because they might cost too much. We're afraid to embrace disarmament because someone else might have a gun. We're afraid to search for truth lest we should find that truth does not exist.

Fear is lack of faith. It takes courage to doubt. It takes faith to doubt. Doubt indicates prior faith. You have to believe in something before you can doubt it. Or, to quote Robert Browning again,

---

[118] Robert Browning, "Bishop Blougram's Apology," in *Poems of Robert Browning,* op. cit., p. 139.

You call for faith:
I show you doubt, to prove that faith exists.
The more of doubt, the stronger faith, I say.[119]

There are so many good and intelligent people in our culture who have rejected Christian faith because they couldn't believe this or that about it, so many really intelligent young people in high school and university who, because they can't believe that the world was created in seven days or that Jesus turned water into wine, have rejected the whole of the Gospel and thrown the baby out with the bath water. Yet they have never gone on to question the alternatives, never begun to doubt their doubts.

So go ahead. Question your beliefs. Attack what you were taught in Sunday School or what you hear from TV evangelists—but follow through to the logical conclusion: go on to question your questions, to question your doubts, to doubt the alternatives. I daresay you may find the alternatives to faith more difficult to hold than faith itself.

At least, that's how it happened for me. After a long and intense search for meaning and purpose in my own life, I came in the end to the great either/or: either life is meaningless and purposeless and love and joy are illusionary, or else at the center of life there beats the heart of the loving God whom Jesus called *Abba*, Father. When I tried to examine the evidence, all the evidence, I found that it was more reasonable to say, however hesitantly, "I believe."

Jesus told the story (Luke 11:5-13) about the man who, in midnight desperation, went to a neighbor's house looking for food for a guest who had come unexpectedly. The neighbor, who had gone to bed, grumpily refused to help him. But because he was so desperate, the midnight visitor kept pounding on the door until he had the whole house awake and in an uproar. There was nothing to do to get rid of him but to come down and give him some food.

And, said Jesus, that is what your search must be like. "Seek, and you shall find. Ask, and it will be given you. Knock, and the door will be opened."

---

[119] Browning, "Bishop Blougram's Apology," op. cit., p. 146.

It sounds so easy when you say it like that. But in the Greek, the meaning is much more intense. The emphasis is on *persistence* in seeking, in asking and knocking. It is saying, "Go on seeking until you find. Keep on asking until you receive. Knock and keep on knocking, even though your arm grows heavy and your knuckles become sore and bloody."

Go on staring into the mystery of the sky, asking all the questions. Look into the abyss, the seemingly black void which we always fear is at the heart of life. Don't just glimpse at it and turn away, running back to the shelter of some false faith. Look right into the heart of it.

You may discern there the form of a cross, and hear the heartbeat of the One whom Jesus called *Abba*, Father.

> I found Him not in world or sun,
> Or eagle's wing, or insect's eye:
> Nor thro' the questions men may try,
> The petty cobweb's we have spun:
>
> If e'er when faith had fall'n asleep,
> I heard a voice "Believe no more!"
> And heard an ever-breaking shore,
> That tumbled in the Godless deep;
>
> A warmth within the breast would melt
> The freezing reason's colder part,
> And like a man in wrath, the heart
> Stood up and answer'd, "I have felt!"
>
> No, like a child in doubt and fear:
> But that blind clamour made me wise.
> Then was I as a child that cries,
> But, crying, knows his father near.[120]

Of course, while I assert it is easier to believe in God than to believe that it is all a fortuitous linking of circumstances, there still hangs the question: Can God be good? How can one believe in the goodness of God in a world of natural disaster and such terrible human injustice and oppression? Here is the problem with which

---

[120] Tennyson, "In Memoriam", CXXIII, op. cit., p. 485.

the Book of Job wrestles, and wrestles mightily. Let's take a look there before we move on.

The Story of Job

"There was a man in the land of Uz ..."

So it begins, what Thomas Carlyle called "one of the grandest things ever written with pen... There is nothing written, I think, in the Bible or out of it, of equal literary merit." He called it "a noble book," and described it an "all men's book! It is our first, oldest statement of the never-ending problem—man's destiny and God's ways with him here in this earth."[121]

"... a man in the land of Uz."

No one can be certain just where "Uz" may have been located. It was probably a desert region southeast of Palestine (note Jeremiah 25:19 ff. and Lamentations 4:21). It doesn't matter where, really, for Uz is everywhere where people suffer, looking out from tight and frightened souls to beseech heaven for an answer—"Why?"

"There was a man in the land of Uz whose name was Job."

No wizard of Uz this man, content with magic's false tricks or any rational slight of hand; just a very human being looking for an honest answer to his questions. The fathers of piety around him spoke of the even-handed justice of God, who blessed the righteous and cursed the careless. It was part of the religious dogmatism of the time. "None but the most impious would dare to question it," said Job's friends, his "comforters." But Job smouldered at their words and protested that what they said just wasn't true, didn't stand up to the facts of life. He wouldn't be content with the glib, easy answers they were always giving people when trouble came upon them.

---

[121] Thomas Carlyle, *Heroes and Hero Worship, and the Heroic in History,* A. L. Burt Company, Publishers, New York, no date, p. 57.

And he stood up alone to do his battle, against a wide unanswering sky. Not for a moment will he truckle, let Omnipotence do what it will. He cannot prevail, but not an inch will he yield.[122]

"There was a man...!"

And so begins the Book of Job.

You may know something of the story, how this ancient sheik of the desert, a man of honour and wealth, in a series of what the insurance companies might call 'acts of God,' lost his property, his family, and his health. He was left in poverty, childless, and sitting upon a dung-heap digging at his terrible, loathsome, itching, stinking sores with an old piece of pottery.

The Book of Job, as we have it in our Bible, seems to have sprung from an ancient folk-tale of the desert. Into this primitive tale has been inserted, at a later date, long and formal arguments between Job and his comforters. This part is poetry, some of the greatest poetry and most powerful imagery ever penned. The prose story forms much of the first and latter chapters.

THE "PATIENCE OF JOB"

Well, what of this story of a man who has become a proverb as we speak of 'the patience of Job?'

That's perhaps the most obvious thing to say—it's not a lesson in patient endurance or long-suffering. Read further than chapter two and you will see that Job was not at all a patient individual. He argued vehemently against the reasoning of his friends, demanding of heaven an accounting for the injustice done him.

And injustice it was. This is the point of the story. Job was a righteous man. This, his comforters tried their best to deny. "All suffering is punishment for sin," they said. "Job is suffering, therefore Job must have sinned."

But Job protested that he had not sinned. He acknowledged his faults; he knew he had them as all people have faults. But he had done nothing that he should be singled out for torture in this manner. He knew that he had been as good as other people, better

---

[122] Paul Scherer in *The Interpreter's Bible* on Job 1:1, Abingdon Press, New York & Nashville, 1954, Vol. III, p. 877f.

than most. "If I had been unfaithful to my wife, unfair to my servants, lacking in concern for the poor and not caring for my heritage, a liar or a cheat, then I would deserve punishment," said Job (in chapter 31). But he hadn't, and that's what made it all so hard to understand.

And so, with great *im*patience, he demanded of heaven an accounting. "Oh that I knew where I might find Him...! I would lay my case before Him, and fill my mouth with arguments" (Job 23:3-4). In fact, it appears to have been Job's very impatience which led to his moment of truth in eyeball-to-eyeball confrontation with the Almighty.

NO NEAT ANSWER

In this strange and subtle story, there is no neat intellectual answer that knows nothing of pain, no facile response to the problem of human suffering. It is Job's comforters who come giving easy answers to the great problems of human existence—and their answers are, one by one, refuted because of their inadequacies. "Miserable comforters, all of you," Job cried. "Why do you think you must speak to me with endless windy words? I could speak as you do if I were in your place and you were in mine" (chapter 16:1-4).

How often ministers sit with those in grief and hear them ask "Why?" We wish that we could give an answer. But the important thing is just to be there, to "be with" as in the word Immanuel, meaning "God with us." In such situations, one must beware above all else the easy, the facile, answer.

Once I visited an old man, a Scot, whose only son had recently been killed. He was literally buried alive in a construction accident. The old man had just come from a neighbour's house and was very, very angry. The neighbour had told him, "It was God's will." But he wasn't satisfied! "What does she know about God's will?" he kept saying. "What does she know?"

When the blow comes, it's not the philosophical answer, not the neat intellectual explanation of the problem, which we seek and need.

In fact, in one sense, there's no answer given in the Book of Job to the question "Why do the righteous suffer?" The argument breaks down, no one seems to have an answer; and then, like the *deus ex machina* of Greek drama,[123] God comes storming in, flexing His muscles and shouting "out of the whirlwind" about His greatness and power. On a superficial reading, God seems to be trying to frighten Job into shutting up, to overawe or overwhelm him because even God doesn't have the answer.

THE ANSWER WHICH IS NO ANSWER

And yet there seems to be more to it than that. Job doesn't just shut up. The strange thing is that Job seems finally somehow content. Something in that tumultuous experience, face to face with the Almighty, quieted his questions and somehow gave him his answer—and Job comes to understand something he had never understood before.

Perhaps it was that, through this experience, he came to a first-hand experience of God's greatness and grace. "I had heard of Thee by the hearing of the ear," he cried, "but now my eye sees Thee" (chapter 42:4). Job realized that the most important thing in life is that a person know the living God. For then you're lifted out of yourself to find Life, abundant Life, Life with a capitol "L."

Martin Buber wrote,

> The only answer Job receives is God's nearness, that He knows God again. Nothing is explained, nothing adjusted, wrong has not become right, nor cruelty kindness, but God is near.[124]

No justification is possible, only "the nearness of God." And the one who cries for justice must "lay his hand upon his mouth." When Job demanded, "Let the Almighty answer me"(chapter 31:35), the answer of the Almighty was far different from the answer Job expected.

> (For) the divine answer is always different from human expectations. From the whirlwind Yahweh does not answer questions; He asks them.[125]

---

[123] A popular spectacle in Greek drama was the appearance of a god at the end of the play who seemed to fly in from the wings. The actor would be suspended from a crane (*mechane*), hence the expression "a god out of the machine."

[124] ibid.

There is something that comes out of our suffering and grief, there face to face with the Almighty. It's not an answer; it's more a challenge and a demand. But through your suffering, you are lifted out of yourself and you come to see life, your life and all life, as you have never seen it before—almost as if with a cosmic vision. As from a great height, you look down upon the ages of human history, the travail and the injustice, the momentary triumph, and the short-lived joy.

And it's not meaningless. In it all, you sense a great heart beating, an infinite Spirit sharing the suffering, knowing the pain, labouring, working, brooding, yearning, agonizing to bring forth the reality of righteousness, truth, and love.

You lay your hand on your lips, for across it all, across the spot where the little girl was killed, across the pioneer cemetery with its grim tally and the sick child crying in agony, across all of this falls the shadow of a cross, and you see things in a new light— the light of God's eternal love! Through your suffering and grief, you just *know*, as you have never known anything before, and nothing can separate you from it ever again.[126]

Job, who had been asserting his own righteousness with so much vehemence to his friends, now, before God, lays his hand on his mouth and says, "Therefore, I repent."[127] It was not because his assertions were incorrect, nor his defence of himself in the face of the comforters' judgments unjustified, but because the answer was so big and profound and true that there was nothing more to say.

Here is simply the story of a good and righteous man who, through his own suffering and sorrow, came to a knowledge of God and an understanding of life not given him before. He was raised out of the prison of the provincial narrowness of his comforters, out of his own limited perspective, lifted onto the windy heights from which he could see the panorama of the universe; torn out of himself to discover the world of God.

---

[125] Samuel Terrien in *The Interpreter's Bible*, op. cit., p. 902

[126] I am speaking here of our understanding of suffering as seen from the perspective of Christian faith, not that Job understood his suffering in the light of Jesus' suffering and death.

[127] Meaning, in this case, to "change one's mind or to reverse one's former judgment." (See *A Theological Wordbook of the Bible*, ed. Alan Richardson, The MacMillan Company, New York, 1953, p. 191.)

That's the story. It begins with "a man in the land of Uz" and it ends with a man in the world of God. That's the difference.

> As the marsh-hen secretly builds on the watery sod,
> Behold I will build me a nest on the greatness of God!
> I will fly in the greatness of God as the marsh-hen flies,
> In the freedom that fills all the space 'twixt the marsh and the
>   skies.
> By so many roots as the marsh-grass sends into the sod,
> I will heartily lay me a-hold of the greatness of God.[128]

Is not God's will for us that we should, like Job, rise out of the narrow, provincial prison of our self-concern to realize the wonderful world of God? To know God's presence even in the midst of pain, the amazing nearness of God even in our grief? Is not this what God wants, above all else, that we know God's love? Our greatest need, in time of grief, is that we realize the presence of that loving Spirit whose love is so vast, so great, that it would share our sorrow, even suffering and death, on the cross.

Justice and Love

Poet Archibald MacLeish, two-time Pulitzer Prize winner, took the story of Job as the basis of a verse-play about a twentieth century businessman, J.B., who suffers disaster after disaster.

In the closing scene of the play, J.B.'s wife, Sarah, returns to him:

J.B.: Curse God and die, you said to me.

Sarah: Yes.
       You wanted justice, didn't you.
       There isn't any. There's the world …
       Cry for justice and the stars
       Will stare until your eyes sting. Weep,
       Enormous winds will thrash the water.
       Cry in sleep for your lost children,
       Snow will fall…
       Snow will fall.

---

[128] From "The Marshes of Glynn," by Sidney Lanier, quoted by in *The Interpreter's Bible,* op. cit., p. *907.*

J.B.:   Why did you leave me alone?

Sarah: I loved you.
         I couldn't help you anymore.
         You wanted justice and there was none –
         Only love.[129]

We cry for justice, but our deepest need is love.

OUR CONCERN FOR JUSTICE

Our capacity for order is one thing that makes our lives human. We analyze and categorize and put things "in their place." Parents know the struggle it is to get teenagers to keep their bedrooms tidy, but we all know, young and old, that it is a continual struggle to keep some degree of order and stability in our own lives. We all have a "junk drawer" or a Fibber Magee's closet.[130]

Related to our capacity for order is our ability to achieve some measure of justice in our relations with others, some measure of "fair play" and "equality under the law."

We are willing to allow others a place in the world, even perhaps to accord them "equality under the law," but we want to believe in return that we will get what is coming to us—"fair is fair"—and we want our efforts to bring a worthwhile reward. We may be kind to those who are kind to us, but if we are unfairly injured we want retribution. If we are cheated, slandered or insulted, we want to retaliate.

We have an expectation that good should be rewarded and evil punished. So, if we work hard all month, we expect a reasonable return at the end of the month. If we lead a quiet, honest, and moral life, we want to believe that in return we will have peace and security in our time on earth and assurance of eternal bliss in the life to come.

The rules of fair play on the sports field and even in children's games, the expectation of some reasonable measure of justice in business and community life, these are written deep within our

---

[129] Archibald MacLeish, op. cit. p. 151. The play ends on a disappointing and purely humanistic note, with Sarah calling on J.B. to "Blow on the coal of the heart."

[130] For those too young to remember (and that's most of us), this is a reference to a radio comedy program of the 1940's called "Fibber Magee and Molly." When Fibber opened the door to the hall closet, great noise over the radio would signify piles of possessions falling into the hall. It always got a laugh.

collective psyche. We seek to establish them, and even to enforce them as "laws" of our society. These are the means by which we maintain some minimal order in what we call "civilization."

Religion, to most people, is belief in such a moral order in the universe. When we see the wicked living in prosperous contentment or immoral persons evidently quite carefree and happy, we feel that our very belief in God is threatened. We cry for justice—an eye for an eye, and a tooth for a tooth.

THREE MORAL REALMS

There are three moral realms, or levels of justice, in our human experience. The first, the lowest level, is the realm of nature, "red in tooth and claw," whose law is the law of the jungle. This is the realm of no morality, of *amorality*. Here, the individual creature seeks to preserve its existence at the expense of the existence of other creatures, by preying on them.

The second realm is the realm of history, the realm of our ordinary human life. This is the realm of our common morality and law, of restricted retribution and balanced, evenhanded justice—"an eye for an eye and a tooth for a tooth." In this realm, we may transcend the law of the jungle.

By either tacit or enforced agreement, either fair play, the established and largely unconscious rules of the game, or by the legislated and enforced laws of human society, we contain and control the instinct for self-aggrandizement at the expense of others. We ensure our own existence by allowing others to ensure their existence in some equal measure, the mutuality of restricted retribution, and so provide some measure of security and welfare in our common life.

The "Deuteronomic Code,"[131] with its prescription of "an eye for an eye and a tooth for a tooth," was actually an advance over the law of the jungle and even over the tribal custom of unlimited retribution. By these more primitive standards, if someone knocked out one of your teeth, you attempted to get fuller recompense by knocking out all his teeth. Then would ensue an ever-escalating scale of revenge that would result in an inter-tribal

---

[131] The copy or reiteration of the Judaic laws in the book of Deuteronomy.

bloodbath—murder, rape, and mayhem, probably resulting in the decimation of one of the tribes involved.

The law of "an eye for an eye and a tooth for a tooth" put a limit to the retribution within the tribal units of Israel. The result was a system of balanced or proximate justice in the society, by which not only one's own life and goods were secured, but the very institutions and order of the society were maintained.

There is a third realm of moral order. This is the realm of grace. This is the realm of forgiveness and sacrificial love, which Nicholas Berdyaev called the "morality beyond morality."[132] Here, we enter into a realm that transcends our normal moral understanding, a type of relationship that both fulfills and annuls our common conceptions of justice.

A mother does not say to her baby, or a father to his two-year-old daughter, "You haven't earned your keep this week, therefore you shall not eat!" Wife and husband don't sit down at the end of the month and try to make certain that the amount they have each spent should balance off to the dollar. (If they do, their marriage is in trouble). Where there is this sacrificial love, the second realm of "an eye for an eye and a tooth for a tooth," while still important, is not given primary consideration.

Where there is forgiveness and sacrificial love, we often "turn the other cheek." We get up at four o'clock in the morning to drive one of our children to hockey practice. We give up a trip to Hawaii so that a daughter can wear braces on her teeth.

This is the realm of "grace," where our common concepts of morality and justice are largely irrelevant. They are both fulfilled and destroyed, because they are transcended.

Suppose two neighbours have a dispute over a boundary line. One threatens to sue the other. If the response is that of forgiving love—"John, that eighteen inches of land is not worth hard feelings between us. If it means that much to you, take it!"—then the demands of law and of justice are both fulfilled and transcended by such a simple act.

---

[132] Quoted by Reinhold Niebuhr, "The Providence of God," p. 15, in *Justice and Mercy*, ed. Ursula Niebuhr, Harper & Row, Publishers, New York, Hagerstown, San Francisco, London, 1974, pp. 16f.

And paradoxically, it is in this caring and forgiving love, the love of a parent for a child for instance, that the self finds its most complete fulfillment. In ceasing to care for itself, in giving of itself to another, in forgetting itself, the self transcends itself and finds its own most complete fulfillment.[133]

It should always be a sobering thought that Christ was crucified not by the forces of human evil but by human systems of justice and order. Members of the Sanhedrin were not evil, but rather the most revered and trusted members of the Hebrew nation. Roman justice was not simply trivial and barbaric. Though it was often brutal in its enforcement, it was the best system of justice that the human race had known to that time.

The people whom Christ most condemned were not the supposedly bad people of the period, but the good people—the most moral and religious people, typified by the "scribes and Pharisees," professional lay exponents and teachers of the Law, the *Torah*.[134] These were righteous men, men of justice, who fought every evidence of evil in themselves and in their society. They were meticulously careful in observance of the Law, to ensure that every regulation was regarded and that precise retribution was exacted according to the prescriptions laid down.

Jesus said of them that they would tithe even the tiny seeds of garden herbs—mint, and anise and cumin! They would rather see an animal, or even a human being, suffer than condone the breaking of Sabbath regulations.

But people who are so strictly righteous lack the highest virtue of all. They lack the quality of mercy. They cannot forgive, and because they cannot forgive, they cannot love. It was precisely for this reason that Jesus condemned them—they were so rigidly righteous that they could neither give mercy, nor receive it. They were willing to sacrifice love for justice.

"Except your righteousness *exceed* that of the scribes and Pharisees," Jesus said to His disciples, "you shall in no way enter

---

[133] We must always remember that Jesus' commandment is to love another *as one loves one's self*. God's love may be limitless and unconditional, but in human love there must of course be limits and some proximate justice.

[134] The Torah was the detailed regulations found in the first five books of the Bible, called the Pentateuch, which guided Jewish life and ensured a right relationship with God.

the kingdom of heaven" (Matthew 5:20)—a saying that must have distressed them, for surely no one could have been more righteous than the scribes and Pharisees. But the scribes and Pharisees, for all their righteousness, lacked that forgiving and sacrificial love, "the morality beyond morality," which is both the fulfillment and the annulment of the Law. And for lacking this, Jesus condemned them. For love fulfills every concept of justice and rises above it, rendering it obsolete and unnecessary.

We cry for justice, but our greatest need is love. It is in loving one another beyond the bounds of justice that we find fulfillment, and it is in knowing the love of God, revealed in Jesus and His cross, that we may find our greatest comfort.

Can God Be Good?

We started with the question, "Can God be good?" How can one claim to believe and trust in the goodness of God in the face of the ambiguities and injustices of life, especially the suffering of the helpless and the innocent?

We considered the alternative—no God, no faith, no belief— and I suggested "doubting our doubts," that we may find that it is in fact more difficult to believe in nothing.

We looked at the Book of Job, one of the oldest and most powerful expressions of the problem, one that seems to provide an answer that is no answer—that *the goodness of God, which is the problem, is the only answer to the problem.*

This goodness surpasses our common understanding of human goodness. We tend to think in terms of law and justice. This goodness is the goodness of selfless and sacrificial love. Here is the goodness we, like Job, find face to face with the Almighty, a goodness that we may find even in the face of terrible injustice, in the suffering of innocent children. The light of the cross shows us the presence of a suffering God, present with us, seeking to work out His purpose in a world gone wrong.

This, of course, is easy to say sitting in a comfortable chair in a comfortable room in reasonable health. But the reality of the situation for someone who faces pain, injustice, and death, is quite different. How do we believe in the goodness of God when our child is fighting a terrible and losing battle with one of the many forms of cancer? How do we find the comfort of God's presence when a young wife, the mother of three children, is killed in a motor accident caused by a drunken driver?

It's one thing to "believe" in the goodness of God as an intellectual assertion. It's something else to "know" in one's heart the comfort of God's love. The way we come to know the comfort of God's presence is, perhaps surprisingly, through the process we call grief. Through our grief, we may rise out of the provincial prison of our pain and rise to live and love again.

Good Grief!

In life, there is not one death, but many—many little losses and griefs, and of course some big ones. Any experience of death or loss causes us to grieve. Loss of loved ones, most certainly. But also the loss of a job, or leaving a place where we have lived for many years and which we have called "home." Children know grief when a pet dies, and they sometimes want to have a "funeral service." Teenagers know grief when a teenage romance breaks up, and anyone who has experienced the break-up of marriage or the loss of a child has known intense grief.

Each of us experiences grief to some extent, for grief is the experience of death, of loss, of separation. Something or someone we love is taken from us. Something we value is destroyed. We face failure and ridicule. We face our own suffering, our own death. We know grief. Physical symptoms may result—a tightness in the throat or chest, or a heavy feeling in the stomach that won't go away. Food tastes like sand, the simplest tasks and decisions are difficult. We have no will to live, and life seems empty. God seems gone.

Grief is a very difficult experience, but grief itself is not bad! It's the death, the loss, the separation, that is bad. The experience of it may be painful, but grief itself is good! Grief is the healing process through which we recover from the death, the loss, and the separation.

COMFORT THROUGH THE BIBLE

The Bible speaks much of grief, and its resources are extraordinarily rich and can give great comfort.

The "Shepherd Psalm" (Psalm 23) is common to the Protestant, Catholic and Jew, and has been a source of comfort to hundreds of thousands of people down through the years. Also Jesus' words on the night before He died, as recorded in the Gospel of John: "Let not your hearts be troubled, you believe in God, trust also me. In my Father's house are many rooms, I go to prepare yours for you" (John 14:1f.) Your room, in your Father's house!

There's Paul's great assurance of resurrection in I Corinthians 15: "If for this life only we have hope in Christ, we are of all people most to be pitied. But in fact, Christ has been raised from the dead, the first fruits of those who have died" (I Corinthians 15: 19-20). And there is the wonderful picture of the holy city of God: "He will wipe away every tear from their eyes. Death will be no more; mourning and crying and pain will be no more, for these former things will have passed away" (Revelation 21:4).

In the Bible, in the midst of grief, there is always hope, even in the face of death itself, for our trust is in the ultimate and the Eternal, Almighty God.

We would not have you grieve as those who have no hope. We believe that Jesus died and rose again. So too will God bring those who died in Christ to be with Him (I Thessalonians 4:13-14).

Blessed are those who mourn, for they shall be comforted (Matthew 5:4).

GRIEF IS NATURAL!

The first thing that must be said about grief is that it is natural. Grief is the normal human reaction to loss, separation, or death.

People sometimes feel that it's wrong to grieve. They speak of grief as though it indicates a lack of faith. They say that if their loved ones are in heaven, they should be happy for them. "I'm only grieving for myself," they say, as though it were wrong. It's not wrong; it's natural.

It's true, of course. We do weep for ourselves. But there's nothing wrong with that. We are the ones who are left, alone, feeling the pain of separation. Grief is the price of our love! Because we have loved someone, we feel the pain of grief when they're gone. If we would avoid grief, we should never open ourselves to love!

> He' we never lov'd sae kindly,
> Ha' we never lov'd sae blindly,
> Never met—nor never parted –
> We ha' ne'er been broken hearted.[135]

But while the cost is great, is not the alternative so much more forbidding: the cold and isolated heart that will not allow itself to love for fear of the pain of grief?

We should not add feelings of guilt to our burden of grief. Grief is normal. It's natural. In fact, to lose someone or something you have cherished and not grieve, that would be most unnatural!

GRIEF IS NECESSARY!

Grief is natural, but it is also necessary!

A cousin once told me of her experience. Her mother had died the year before, in her eighties, after a long and hard struggle with cancer. At the time, she did not cry or own great sorrow, but rather felt some sense of relief that her mother's pain was over. She believed that her mother was in a better place. It was one year later, on a beautiful autumn afternoon, when she was on a drive with her husband and children. Suddenly she began to cry. She cried and cried and cried—over her mother's death, the glory and the shortness of life, and love of her family.

We can't stifle it or bury it inside us! It's better to acknowledge our grief and deal with it in as constructive a way as possible. Otherwise, it will assume some pathological expression—we develop ulcers or worse, or get very angry at everything and everyone and become quite unfit to live with.

The inevitability of grief is shown in the customs our race has developed to deal with it. The practices of what we call "mourning" go back to the earliest days of our humanity. Signs of grief in

---

[135] *The Complete Poetical Works of Robert Burns, with a biographical sketch by Nathen Haskell Dole*, Thomas Y. Crowell and Co., Publishers, New York, 1900, pp. 260-261.

ancient graves are the earliest and surest indications of humanity in the evolution of the human race.

Some mourning customs are very helpful, but sometimes they become fixed customs that have lost their relevance and no longer bring comfort. When such customs lose their meaning, they become mere formalities, even absurdities. Years ago, it was a common custom to have an open casket at a funeral service, and after the service everyone would parade past the casket "to view the remains." Some people may have found it helpful, having to face the reality of death in this way, but many did not.

Back in the place where my family came from, there was a woman named "Lizzie" who made it a practice to attend all funerals in the area and take her place among the mourners, though she wasn't part of the family or even a friend of the deceased. When the time came to parade to the casket and "view the remains," Lizzie would go into her act—wailing and crying and carrying on. Local teenagers would attend the service, sitting in the back row to watch Lizzie in her act. What may once have been a helpful custom had, through Lizzie's antics, become absurd.

Grief is very individual, and in my experience no one can tell someone else what he or she should do about it. While one person wants lots of people around, another wants to be alone or to sit quietly with one or two friends. One person will get very busy, while another feels incapable of doing anything. Early in my ministry, I was called to a home where the wife and mother, a woman in her early sixties, had died suddenly. The husband was very businesslike, wanting to get all the details of the funeral arranged while her body was hardly out of the house. I started to get angry, until I realized that he was in shock and that this was the way he had to deal with it.

Two things that seem most helpful in our grief are tears and talk. These seem to be nature's way of helping us to deal with our grief. Tears are not a sign of weakness or a cause of shame. It's one way we are given to express our grief, and it may be necessary to weep for the Spirit of God to heal us.

And sometimes, when someone is grieving, they want to talk and talk about their loss. Yes, if you don't share the extent of their grief, listening can be burdensome; but for the person who bears the grief, it's necessary.

A time of grief can become a time of shared memories. I have often sat with a family at a time of grief and have watched and listened as the stories are told. Sometimes the memories are funny and there may be laughter. Then there will be a long silence, after which the talk will start again. One can sense the healing begin to take place.

BUT GRIEF IS NOT THE LAST WORD!

While grief may be necessary, it's not necessarily the last word! "In the midst of life we are in death!" says the funeral service of the Anglican Prayer Book. But it's also true to say that in the midst of death we are in life!

Many times I have stood at a grave side with family and friends of the deceased. Death is the reality we face, but all around us are signs of life; the grass, the trees, a birdsong. Even in the midst of winter there is the sound of nearby life—of traffic, of children calling to one another, or a plane overhead. It always seems to remind me of the promise of the Gospel, that life is greater than death, and life is the final reality.

Is this not why hope is such an essential ingredient if our grief is to be "good grief?" Beyond the losses and separations of life, all of life's "death experiences," even in the face of death itself, there is the possibility of healing and even wholeness in the promises of God in the Gospel.

> We would not have you ignorant, brothers and sisters, concerning those who are asleep, that you should not grieve as those who have no hope. For since we believe that Jesus died and rose again, even so, through Jesus, God will bring those who died to be with Him (I Thessalonians 4:13-14).

Grief without hope! It seems to me that must be very terrible.

Isn't this why *faith* is so important? Without faith, can we finally have hope? Faith and hope may give us the courage to pick up the pieces and move on, even if it's just barely putting one foot ahead of the other. Tears and anger, even withdrawal, may come back again and again, but not with the same devastating impact. Gradually, we gain strength and begin to live again.

In a little book, *Good Grief*, Granger Westberg, a Lutheran minister, writes,

I am convinced of the importance of keeping at the task of nurturing one's faith because I have seen how such people demonstrate greatness under trial. Conversely, I now have seen what happens to people who have not taken seriously the necessity of working at their faith when life was good. These people seem unprepared to handle even the smaller losses which all of us face from time to time....

At the time of great loss, people who have a mature faith give evidence of an uncommon relationship with God. They demonstrate an uncommon inner sense of strength and poise which grows out of their confidence that such a relationship with God can never be taken away from them. With such a basic philosophy they can face any earthly loss with the knowledge that they still have not lost everything. They still have God on whom to rely. I have come to see that this way of looking at life makes an amazing difference in the quality of the grief experience. It can actually become *good grief!*[136]

THE DEMONIC DYNAMIC IN GRIEF

It seems to me that there is a dynamic element in grief that I would call demonic, and which makes it difficult for faith. At the very time when we are, consciously and desperately, crying out to God for comfort and help, there is, on a deeper and unconscious level, anger at what has happened, and God is where the buck stops. On one level of our being, the conscious level, we call out to God for help, while on the unconscious level we would like to wipe God out of our life and out of the whole universe. God must be the one finally responsible for our loss and the subsequent pain. There is a conflict going on deep within us. We both cry to God for help and also blame God for our loss.

This is why, common to grief, we experience the sense of emptiness. God seems gone. We pray, we cry out in our anguish, but sense no answer or presence. The only thing we can do, it seems, is persist—keep on knocking on the door even though our knuckles are bruised and sore, keep on asking though the silence mocks our prayer, keep on seeking. Keep on! Keep on!

---

[136] Granger E. Westberg, *Good Grief: a Constructive Approach to the Problem of Loss*, Fortress Press, Philadelphia, 1962, pp. 50 & 51.

Here are two accounts of personal grief, one of them seemingly spectacular in its result, the other more like the experience of most of us.

Author Catherine Marshall's *Christy* is based on the experience of her mother, who left her comfortable city home at the age of 19 to teach school in the Smoky Mountains of East Tennessee. There she came to know and love the wild mountains and the people with their fierce pride, their dark superstitions, their terrible poverty, and their yearning for beauty and truth. She found her own faith challenged many times, but most deeply in the death of a young mother (with the mountain name of "Fairlight") with whom she developed a deep, loving, and supportive friendship. When a typhoid epidemic swept through the community, and Fairlight died, Christy was left in grief.

> It must have been about the eighth day after the funeral that the world came back into focus. … Then I knew how sorely I had been wounded. This was no ache but a wild, searing pain boring into my vitals, piercing every thought.

> I doubt that my torment was altruistic. Probably most grief contains a large measure of self-pity; mine no exception. Clawing questions gave me no peace. What if I...? Why didn't I...? If only I had not failed!

> Beyond that, however, my resentment was directed at God Almighty. I wondered why one person and not another. Why not someone not quite bright, or someone old and crippled, whose children were grown and whose life was almost over anyway? Why were the good and the beautiful so ruthlessly plucked? ...

> No, it made no sense to me. Justice was justice. Apparently we could count on no justice in this life: heaven's ways are surely not our ways. In my rebellion I was not certain that I wanted any part of such a heaven—that is, if there is any life after this one, for doubts now gnawed like rats at the fabric of my faith....

> Each night sleep came only with exhaustion. And even then I tossed—hot and restless—pursued by dreams that had a nightmarish quality. Often I would awaken with a throbbing head and aching legs....

> After a restless night, I got up shortly before dawn one Saturday morning, dressed hastily, and tiptoed out of the house. As I reached my woodland retreat on Coldsprings Mountain, the sun

was just rimming the tip of the far ranges. The sky was rosy, with streaks of golden light filtering through the trees. Dewdrops still glistened on the leaves. The woods were quiet, so quiet, save for my own footfall and an occasional bird call.

It was beautiful morning. My eyes saw the beauty, but I could not respond to it. The anger against God that I had felt at the funeral, for which I had gotten no satisfactory answers, was compounded now. God? Where was God? Far way? Indifferent? Never there at all? A figment of wishful imagining?

Or if there, why had God not done something to prevent her death? ...

So the bitter thoughts rolled and seethed inside me. Suddenly, sitting there on the hillside, I remembered the presentiment that had come to me the day we had climbed to the top of the mountain. Then, with intuitive knowing, I had been sure that indeed it does matter how we live our lives, that there is One who cares. Thinking of that, I knew that it was wrong not to speak out my rebellion to the One to whom it was directed. I could at least give God a chance to defend Himself!

Speak it out! Yes, and act it out. It must have been my isolation that gave me the courage to let all constraint go. I heard myself saying aloud, "Why? Why? I've got to know why!" Then on my knees in a bed of dry leaves, I was flailing my fists on the earth....

I don't understand, God! I don't understand. I don't understand death and I don't understand You. Why are You so inscrutable? Why are You so hard to find when the need is greatest? I can't get through to you. I'm asking for help! Am I pleading with a void? Am I?

Gradually I quieted down. The rain of my words ceased. There was no answer immediately. I had not expected there would be. Yet the leafy quietness enfolded me, soothed me. I was aware of a thirst to drink deeply of the silence, the soothing silence....

I decided that I would return again and again to my mountain sanctuary until some response, some insights were given me. Or else! There was always the stark alternative that there would never be any response because I was indeed speaking to nothingness.

I began setting my alarm clock for a quarter of six each morning. Then on the hillside propped against the trunk of my favourite tree, I would watch the sun rise. By the second morning, I stopped hurling invectives verbally and began writing my questions in a notebook. Some of what I wrote bordered on blasphemy. Yet there was a feeling of hard soundness about being honest. If there was a God, life would have to be truth. And in that case, candour—however impertinent—would be more pleasing to God than posturing. Gradually the torment of my grief fell away. In its place was left a great wistfulness and a terrible aloneness.

I opened my Bible and there I found astonishing companionship. Other men and women long ago had asked the identical questions that I was asking. Job too had shaken his fist in the face of heaven as I had there on my hillside.... And I found Psalm after Psalm that had been poured out in the same agony of spirit that I was feeling, set down in naked, unashamed emotion....

Morning after morning I returned to my hillside spot to reach out for the stillness as a thirsty man reaches for a cup of cold water. I had never experienced anything like this before: a silence so complete that it seemed palpable, sensate, an entity in itself.

Yet the quietness was no sterile emptiness. Those who craved oblivion could not have tolerated this. Or those who wanted to escape themselves would flee this....

Now I knew that at the heart of the stillness there was food to feed upon, wisdom to accept, humbly, satisfaction to be quaffed. Irresistibly the silence drew me because it promised that where there was hunger there would also be bread.

And slowly, almost imperceptibly, out of the stillness, my answer started coming—only not in any way I had expected. No effort was made to answer my "why?" Instead, I began to know, incredibly, unmistakably, beyond reason and beyond doubting, that I, Christy Huddleston, was loved—tenderly, totally. Love filled me, washing over me, flowed around me. I did not know what to do with love as strong as this. Back off from its intensity? Embrace it?

My tears flowed. I could not stop them.

Then the thought came: wasn't this the confirmation for which I had asked? This love disclosing itself was no cosmic Creator of a mechanistic universe, for the revelation was intimate, personal. Perhaps the assurance always has to be personal, revealed to the inner person alone—for God insists on seeing us one by one, each a special case.

The world around me was still full of riddles for which my little mind had not been given answers. Nor could I know what the future held. But the fundamental doubt was silenced. I knew now:

God is! I had found my centre, my point of reference. Everything else I needed to know would follow.

That morning, the sun came up in a blaze of glory.[137]

The other account, not so dramatic in its resolution but just as deep in its pain, is that of C. S. Lewis. He tells of his experience when his wife died.

> Meanwhile, where is God! This is one of the most disquieting symptoms. When you are happy, so happy that you have no sense of needing Him, so happy that you are tempted to feel His claims upon you as an interruption, if you remember yourself and turn to Him with gratitude and praise, you will be—or so it feels—welcomed with open arms. But go to Him when your need is desperate, when all other help is vain, and what do you find? A door slammed in your face, and a sound of bolting and double bolting on the inside. After that, silence. You as well turn away. The longer you wait, the more emphatic the silence will become.... Why is He so present a commander in our time of prosperity and so very absent a help in time of trouble?[138]

Lewis tells later of the healing that has taken place, but only after a long, hard, and very gradual struggle.

> Still, there are the two enormous gains—I know myself too well now to call them "lasting." Turned to God, my mind no longer meets that locked door; turned to H., it no longer meets that vacuum—nor all that fuss about my mental image of her. My jottings show something of the process, but no so much as I'd hoped. Perhaps both changes were really not observable. There was no sudden, striking, and emotional transition. Like the warming of a room or the coming of daylight. When you first notice them they have already been going on for some time.[139]

Just as Elizabeth Kübler-Ross wrote about the stages of accepting death,[140] so there are stages of grief. The first is denial of the

---

[137] Catherine Marshall, *Christy,* Spire Books, The Hearst Corporation, New York, 1972, chp. 39, pp. 426ff.

[138] C. S. Lewis, *A Grief Observed*, Bantam Books, New York, 1976, pp. 4-5

[139] Lewis, *A Grief Observed*, p. 71.

[140] Elizabeth Kübler-Ross, *On Death And Dying*, Macmillan Publishing Co., Inc., New York, first paperback edition, 1970.

reality, shock. Then there may be pain, anger, and resistance, which come and go, until finally, with faith and hope, there may be some acceptance of the loss and readiness to return to the demands that God places upon us in our own life.

Through it all, there is a healing Spirit.

The Healing Spirit

We were camping a number of years ago at a friend's place by the shore of Big Bras D'Or Lake on Cape Breton Island. It was a beautiful spot. The previous winter had been a difficult one for me. There were several complicated situations in my congregation that had to be faced and worked through, and the struggles had taken their toll on my spirit, and even on my physical health.

I remember walking by the shore of the lake for a long, long time one night. Brenda and the children were asleep in the tent. It was a warm summer night, the full moon shone across the water to my feet, and I remember the lapping of the little waves along the shore—I remember especially the lapping of the water.

When I went back to bed, it was with a feeling of peace, and I remember coming back from that vacation with a sense of health and wholeness that I had not had for months.

Naturalist Loren Eiseley tells of an incident in his adventures when he saw vividly the healing Spirit at work in all of life. In this case, he witnessed the Spirit of healing at work in the face of the cruelties of nature, an affirmation of life in the face of the reality of death:

> You may put it that I had come over a mountain, that I had slogged through fern and pine needles for half a long day, and that on the edge of a little glade with one long, crooked branch across it, I had sat down to rest with my back against a stump. Through accident I was concealed from the glade, although I could see into it perfectly.
>
> The sun was warm there, and the murmurs of forest life blurred softly away into my sleep. When I awoke, dimly aware of some commotion and outcry in the clearing, the light was slanting down through the pines in such a way that the glade was lit like some vast cathedral. I could see the dust motes of wood pollen in the

long shaft of light, and there on the extended branch sat an enormous raven with a red and squirming nestling in his beak.

The sound that awoke me was the outraged cries of the nestling's parents, who flew helplessly in circles about the clearing. The sleek black monster was indifferent to them. He gulped, whetted his beak on the dead branch a moment and sat still. Up to that point the little tragedy had followed the usual pattern. But suddenly, out of all that area of woodland, a soft sound of complaint began to rise. Into the glade fluttered small birds of half a dozen varieties drawn by the anguished outcries of the tiny parents.

No one dared to attack the raven. But they cried there in some instinctive common misery, the bereaved and the unbereaved. The glade filled with their soft rustling and their cries. They fluttered as though to point their wings at the murderer. There was a dim intangible ethic he had violated, that they knew. He was a bird of death. And he, the murderer, the black bird at the heart of life, sat on there, glistening in the common light, formidable, unmoving, unperturbed, untouchable.

The sighing died. It was then I saw the judgment. It was the judgment of life against death. I will never see it again so forcefully presented.... There, in that silence, the crystal note of a song sparrow lifted hesitantly in the hush. And finally, after painful fluttering, another took the song, and then another, the song passing from one bird to another, doubtfully at first, as though some evil thing were being slowly exorcised. Till suddenly they took heart and sang from many throats joyously together as birds are known to sing. They sang because life is sweet and sunlight beautiful. They sang under the brooding shadow of the raven. In simple truth they had forgotten the raven, for they were the singers of life, and not of death.[141]

The song of birds, I am told, is a statement of identity, a saying "I am here," and of communication, of reaching out to others.

There is a healing Spirit. The Spirit of Jesus is still at work in life, even as He healed the sick and cured those oppressed with evil spirits so many hundreds of years ago by the shores of the Sea of Galilee. This healing Spirit doesn't necessarily act in sudden and miraculous ways as seemed the case in Jesus' day. More often

---

[141] Loren Eiseley, *The Immense Journey*, Vintage Books, a division of Random House, New York, 1946, pp. 173-175.

the Spirit works gradually, sometimes so gradually as to seem imperceptible—until you look back and realize the change that has taken place.

So many times in my ministry I have craved to lay my hands on somebody as Jesus did and see them instantly healed. Perhaps I lacked the faith, the confidence in God's power, to accomplish it. But there have been times I prayed for healing, and have felt the prayer was answered, not necessarily immediately or spectacularly, not always completely or permanently, but effectively.

There was Mrs. Dalling.

My first "pastoral charge" was seven churches in southern New Brunswick near Sussex. The Kennebecasis valley was beautiful, especially when in the late afternoon the sun cast shadows on the surrounding hills. The main point on the charge was Sussex Corner, just outside Sussex.

I had been there for less than two weeks. It was the day of the annual Strawberry Festival at Sussex Corner, a big event and people came from all over the countryside to attend. I was there, putting in an appearance, mixing with the crowd, urging the troops (the women of the congregation) in their efforts, and sampling the strawberry shortcake.

Then someone came up to me and gave me the news: Mrs. Dalling had had a stroke. The doctor said she would not make it to sunset. Would I come? It was my first pastoral crisis.

Not knowing what else to do, I went home and got the home communion set that had been given me as an ordination present. With the communion set containers filled somehow with grape juice and little cubes of bread, I set off for Russell Crowe's place. (Jane, Russell's wife, had been a Dalling.)

Entering the house, I was shown into a first floor bedroom and in the bed I saw a little old woman, quite unconscious. Surrounding the bed were her children, about six of them and all of them *big*—tall, and not one under 250 pounds (at one point, Russell and Jane topped the scales at over 600 pounds). In their shock and grief, they didn't look too friendly, either.

Unsure what was expected, I opened the communion set and prepared to give the unconscious woman communion. After a prayer, I began to repeat the 46th psalm, "God is our refuge and strength…" From the unconscious woman on the bed, a voice seeming from the grave, came the response: "...a very present help in trouble."

I went on to the next verse, "Therefore will I not fear...." Again the response, "...though the earth be removed...." The voice faded.

My attempt to give her communion was quite unsuccessful. Fortunately, it didn't do any harm. In fact, Mrs. Dalling lived far beyond sunset. She quite enjoyed life for more than three years after that day. Finally, though, she died and I had to bury her.

I have never forgotten the mystery of that occasion. Who am I to say that faith was not a central part of that healing occasion, the faith of an old woman who had lived a hard life but who knew the psalm and had no doubt repeated it often, not just in church but also in the quiet of her heart for her own comfort and strengthening?

Some doctors and nurses will tell you that they do not heal. They only provide the circumstances in which healing can take place, but the healing is beyond their power. It was a French surgeon of the sixteenth century, Ambrose Paré, ranked as one of the great surgeons of all time, who would say, "I treated him. God cured him."[142]

There was another time among many in my experience when I was very conscious of God's healing Spirit. A member of my congregation in Fredericton had lost his father to lung cancer. Don was a very good friend and fishing partner. He had been very fond of his father and the two had been close. The father's death affected him deeply.

We walked by ourselves along the shore of the Saint John River, a long walk. I said almost nothing. He talked about his memories of his father, the times they had spent together fishing on the river. We talked of the reality of God in life, even in death, and of the hope of life beyond death.

It was spring, and the river was high. I remember Don's quiet, earnest voice, as well as the long periods of silence, and my own silent prayer for him in his grief. I remember, too, the continuous,

---

[142] John Bartlett, *Famous Quotations: A Collection Of Passages, Phrases And Proverbs Traced To Their Sources In Ancient And Modern Literature,* Fifteenth and 125th Anniversary Edition, ed. Emily Morison Beck, Little, Brown and Company, Boston, Toronto, 1980, p. 162, no.9.

unending flow of the waters, washing, splashing, gurgling, rushing along beside us where we walked.

There is something about water, the eternal ebb and flow of the tides, the ceaseless flow of the river, the lapping of the waves on the shore or the crashing of the surf. There's something healing about water. It helps me to get a sense of the Eternal, even somehow of the eternal "rightness" of what is—not that it is *now* right, but somehow ultimately it becomes right, it is *made right*.

Some philologists claim that the word "abundance" comes from the Latin *ab unda*—meaning literally "from the wave"—the sense of the waves lapping on the shore and the tide coming in, wave after wave, one after another, unending, limitless.

There is an abundance in God, the everlasting, unending, unlimited source of love. It's what John Knox, the New Testament scholar of the last generation, called (in a meditation on Paul's phrase in I Corinthians 1) "the foolishness of God."

> The profuse splendour of a world where diamonds lie hidden in the bowels of the earth and some of the most beautiful flowers bloom in the depths of the jungle, where the most spectacular display of northern lights across the arctic midnight sky may be seen by no one.

> One cannot live long in the world and love it much and still believe that God is only "wise" (in the prudential and pragmatic sense that we give to the word "wisdom"). There is everywhere about us an extravagance, a purposeless profuseness and spleen-dour, which, if it be not proper to call "foolishness" is surely not wisdom (or prudence). The heavens have not been said to declare the wisdom of God, but rather what would appear to be His foolish prodigality, His magnificence, His *glory*! ...

> We are told He knows every star by name—this we can believe, for every separate star is the work of His hand. But that he created each star for some human use or as a means to some end is not necessarily true. The stars do not exist because of their utility. So far as we can see, they exist because God found joy in making them.

> The earth and the heavens in their concrete fullness cannot be explained as planned constructions, as though God followed a blueprint. Their vast profusion seems rather to represent the illimitable freedom, the pure joy, the boundless creativity, the foolishly wasted beauty, of God....

And does not the cross exhibit to us this same foolish, extravagant goodness, this disinterested overflowing love?[143]

Is it not by His high superfluousness we know
Our God? For to equal a need
Is natural, animal, mineral: but to fling
Rainbows over the rain
And beauty above the moon, and secret rainbows
On the domes of deep sea-shells,
And make the necessary embrace of breeding
Beautiful also as fire,
Not even the weeds to multiply without blossoms,
Nor the birds without music:
There is a great humaneness at the heart of things,
The extravagant kindness, the fountain
Humanity can understand, and would flow likewise
If power and desire were perch-mates.[144]

O Jacob, O Israel, how can you say that the Lord doesn't see your troubles and doesn't care? Don't you know by now that the everlasting God, the Creator of the farthest parts of the earth, never grows faint or weary? No one can fathom the depths of God's understanding! He gives power to the faint and strength to the weak.

Even the young become weary and faint, and those who are strong will fall exhausted. But those who wait upon the Lord shall renew their strength. They shall mount up with wings as eagles. They shall run and not be weary. They shall walk, and not faint! (Isaiah 40:27-31)

I think of the cadence and beauty, even the truth and power, of that passage from Ecclesiastes:

For everything there is a season,
*   and a time for everything under heaven:*
a time to be born, and a time to die;
a time to plant, and a time to reap...

There's an ebb and a flow to it, isn't there?

---

[143] John Knox, "The Foolishness of God," *The Union Seminary Quarterly Review*, Union Theological Serminary, New York City, Vol. XIX, no.1, November, 1963, pp. 1-4.

[144] Robinson Jeffers, *The Selected Poetry of Robinson Jeffers*, Stanford University Press, 2001, p. 17.

a time to be born, a time to die;
a time to plant, a time to reap....
(Ecclesiastes 3:1-8)

So that, even though we hate death, we can accept the death of someone we love. Even when death is sudden, premature, and results in great grief, there can be comfort, and even healing. Even though we don't understand any reason for it, we can to some extent transcend our circumstances and accept with the heart what our reasoning cannot grasp. Truly, "God has placed eternity in our hearts... yet not so that we can comprehend it from beginning to end" (Ecclesiastes 3:11).

Jesus said, "I am come that they have life, and have it abundantly." He died on the cross and was raised from the dead that we might know for sure that life and love are greater than death. In light of that, we may trust in the goodness of God. God wills not our destruction, but our good. God's will for us is *life*, abundant life, illimitable life, eternal life.

Even in the face of death, we have something to look forward to. There is a story of a woman who asked to be buried holding a fork in her hand. She explained that often, at church suppers, when the servers took your plate from the main course, they told you to "keep your fork." It meant that the best was yet to come. To her, what lay beyond death was like desert—the best yet to come.

CHAPTER 6

THE HEART'S TRUE HOME

Life After Life

I have long believed in "life after life," even when I didn't believe in God. It goes back to my father's death. He experienced a very slow death. During the last few weeks of his life, it was not easy to tell if he was still living, but when he died, something went out of his body and the body left behind was not my father. I was convinced, and still am, that he continued to live, somehow, someplace.

I was 17 at the time, and if I believed in God at all it was as a pretty remote proposition. But since that time, I have always had the conviction that there is more to this life then we know here.

Belief in life after life is not an escape hatch for unsolved theological riddles or a way for the injustices of this world to be rectified, whether for vindication or redemption. It is a necessity. Human life, as we know it, is a promise, pointing beyond itself for its fulfillment.

We speak of death as the end of life, but we use the word "end" in two ways. One is chronological, our sense of measured time, of clock-time. The end of the week is when the week is past and over. Death, in this sense, means that life is done, gone, over, caput! But we use the word "end" in another way, a teleological sense, a sense of purpose, as when we are building a house and the house is finished and we are ready to move in. We can think of death either way.

I could go on and give rational and theological reasons for my continued belief in life after life, but this is not a matter to be decided by philosophical argument.

Psychiatrist Raymond A. Moody Jr. has examined the reality of some sort of continuing self-conscious existence following death. He interviewed some fifty people who had near-death experiences:[145] "The experiences of persons who were resuscitated after having been thought, adjudged, or pronounced clinically dead by their doctors; the experiences of persons who, in the course of accidents or severe injury or illness, came very close to physical death; the experiences of persons who, as they died, told them to other people who were present, these other persons reported the content of the death experience to me."[146] In her foreword, Elizabeth Kübler-Ross writes, "It is research such as Dr. Moody presents in this book that will enlighten many and will confirm what we have been taught for two thousand years—that there is life after death."

Moody found the stories expressed very similar experiences: "various unusual auditory sensations" and "out of body" experiences. Some looked down to see their own body on the operating table and the tops of the heads of the doctors and nurses struggling to resuscitate the patient. One remarked, "I never knew my doctor had a bald spot on top of his head." Some spoke of going through a dark tunnel, followed by a feeling of peace and well-being, and being met by "ministering spirits," relatives and loved ones meeting them, welcoming them and comforting them. Finally many spoke of coming into the presence of a wonderful "being of light," "a personal being."

> The love and warmth which emanate from this Being ... are utterly beyond words. (One) feels complete surrounded by it, completely at ease and accepted in the presence of this Being.[147]

It was my impression, a generation ago, that many people questioned the reality of some sort of self-conscious existence after death. I find that is still true of many older people. What surprises me is the rebirth of this expectation among younger people. While

---

[145] "I have interviewed in great detail some fifty persons." Raymond A. Moody, Jr., *Life After Life: The Investigation of a Phenomenon – Survival of Bodily Death,* Bantam Books, New York, 1975, p. 17.
[146] ibid., 16.
[147] ibid., 59.

response to Moody's book has been mixed, there is no doubt in my mind that more people today believe in some sort of life after death, some continuing existence.

Life Is a Promise

As far as I am able to know myself, my belief in a continuing self-conscious existence is not a matter of simply desiring the salvation of my soul or the assurance that "I" will have some kind of everlasting life. It is not fear of death, nor fear of hell. It seems to me that life points beyond itself for its fulfillment. This life in itself is never complete. It is either a promise or a cruel joke, and I cannot believe that life, with all its promise, is a cruel joke.

This life we know is like living inside an egg. It has a limited view of things. Seen from the inside of the egg, death seems to be the inevitable end. But what if someone were to crack open the shell and let in the light? Might it not be that outside the shell that enfolds us there is a world more wonderful than our wildest imaginings? No wonder we have Easter eggs as a symbol of resurrection.

There is a parable told by Kahlil Gibran:

> Once when I was living in the heart of a pomegranate, I heard a seed saying, "Some day I shall become a tree, and the wind will sing in my branches and the sun will dance in my leaves, and I shall be strong and beautiful through all the seasons." Then another seed spoke and said, "When I was as young as you, I too held such views, but now that I can weigh and measure things, I see my hopes were in vain." And a third seed spoke also, "I see in us nothing that promises so great a future." And a fourth one said, "But what mockery this life would be without a greater future!"
>
> Another said, "Why dispute what we shall be when we don't even know what we are?" Until at least all were speaking at once and no sense could be discerned at all for the sound of many voices.[148]

---

[148] Kahlil Gibran, *The Madman, His Parables and Poems*, Alfred A. Knopf, New York, 1949, p.p.35-36.

Perhaps we are like seeds in an apple (a fruit more familiar to us than a pomegranate), living in this world of space and time. A seed has little intimation that it may in fact become a great tree, with blossoms and green leaves and spreading branches bearing fruit. It has no idea of the existence of the world that we take for granted— a world of spreading fields, high skies, towering mountains, and wide seas. Yet *we* know that this world is here.

Until the time of the Copernican revolution, people believed in a very small universe centered on this little planet of ours. Since then, we have recognized that the universe is much greater and more vast than our forebears dreamed.

Perhaps there are dimensions of existence greater and more wonderful than anything we have known or presently know. Perhaps we are, indeed, like seeds in an apple. So far, all we have come to know is something of the inside of the apple itself, without as yet any idea of the vast world that may be outside the apple altogether.

> *But someone will ask, "How are the dead raised? With what kind of body do they come?" Fool! What you sow does not come to life unless it dies. And as for what you sow, you do not sow the body that is to be, but a bare seed, perhaps of wheat or of some other grain. But God gives it a body as he has chosen, and to each kind of seed, its own body....*
>
> *So it is with the resurrection of the dead. What is sown is perishable, what is raised is imperishable. It is sown in dishonor, it is raised in glory. It is sown in weakness, it is raised in power. It is sown a physical body, it is raised a spiritual body.* (I Corinthians 15:35-38, 42-44.)

As the wheat grows from the kernel, as the apple tree grows out of the small seed, so the present "physical body" of ours shall be the seed cast into the ground which may become a body far more glorious than anything we can here imagine.

Some would say that such thoughts are only for fairy tales. But maybe fairy tales are pointing us to the ultimate truth. "As far as I know," writes Frederich Buechner, "there has never been an age that has not produced fairy tales!"[149] J.R.R. Tolkien, of *Lord of the Rings* fame and master of fairy tales, writes that the fairy tale,

> ... does not deny the existence of ... sorrow and failure: the possibility that these are necessary to the joy of deliverance; it denies (in the face of much evidence, if you will) universal final defeat, ... giving a fleeting glimpse of Joy, Joy beyond the walls of the world, poignant as grief.[150]

"Joy beyond the walls of the world!" It's the most haunting, powerful, and persistent dream that humanity has ever concocted.

What is the meaning in our own time of "transcendental meditation," "growth groups," "self-realization," and those maharajahs of the so-called "New Age Spirituality"? Are they not indications that we hope to sense, beyond the noise and confusion of the world around us, another world "where the beauty that sleeps within us will come awake at last?"[151]

We send people to the moon and spaceships to Mars and beyond. We build great electronic ears that we train to the skies hoping to catch some whisper from the stars. And those great armadas that float through space or drive through time, on our television set or on our movie screens, are they still in the future yet to come, or from a world that has always been?

The Resurrection of Jesus Christ

Integral to the belief in life beyond death in Christian faith is the resurrection of Jesus.

> If they think they ha' snared our Goodly Fere
> They are fools to the last degree;
> "I'll go to the feast," quo' our Goodly Fere,
> "Though I go to the gallows tree."

---

[149] Frederich Buechner, *Telling the Truth: the Gospel ad Tragedy, Comedy, and Fairy Tale*, Harper San Francisco, 1977, p. 75.

[150] J. R. Tolkien, *The Tolkien Reader*, Ballantine, New York, 1966, pp. 68-69, quoted by Buechner, p. 81.

[151] Buechner, p. 86.

A master of men was the Goodly Fere,
A mate of the wind and sea.
If they think they ha' slain our Goodly Fere
They are fools eternally.[152]

Did Jesus Christ really rise from the dead?

There is no proof, of course, but we do have quite a bit of evidence. And in the face of the evidence, it seems to me that belief in the resurrection of Jesus Christ is not as unreasonable as some would claim. Not that we can explain it. It certainly was not a simple "physical body." That would be resuscitation, not resurrection. It was something more mysterious—a transformed body, a resurrected body, a "spiritual body" (note I Corinthians 15:44).

When we look at the evidence of history, scripture, and of our own hearts, I suggest that belief in the resurrection of Jesus Christ is an entirely reasonable belief.

THE WITNESS OF HISTORY

Someone has said that if there were as much evidence that Julius Caesar had visited America, we would not doubt it. We accept the works of Tacitus and Josephus, historians of the same general period, though they were not firsthand witnesses of the events they recorded. Why should we not accept the works of those who witnessed the event itself, and the words of those who were their close followers?

Indeed, we regard Tacitus as completely reliable, and he wrote some fifty years after the fact. The earliest manuscripts of his works were not found for a thousand years. The Gospels of Matthew, Mark, and Luke were written thirty or forty years after the event, and we have manuscripts dating back to 150 AD.

In the second chapter of the Book of Acts, we read of Peter's sermon on the day of Pentecost. The sermon is presented as though it is quoting Peter directly, for no doubt it had been told and retold hundreds of times. In fact, it is regarded as a prototype of the message the early church took into the world. Central to that message was the reality of the resurrection.

---

[152] From "Ballad of the Goodly Fere," by Ezra Pound. *A Little Treasury of Modern Poetry,* (Revised Edition, ed. Oscar Williams, New York, Charles Scribner's Sons, 1952, pp. 225-226.

This was their Gospel, the "Good News" that Jesus, who had been crucified, was raised from the dead. Peter repeated it three times—"This Jesus whom you crucified, God has raised!" This was the central point of the message. There was therefore a new hope, a new life, a new age!

The style of the witness is itself so simple and straightforward that it commands confidence. There is no evidence of sophistry or any intent to deceive. It seems quite evident that the writers themselves believed implicitly what they wrote, or why else would they have endured hardship, persecution, suffering, and death?

Simon Greenleaf was head of Harvard Law School near the middle of the nineteenth century. Turning his legal mind to the New Testament witness to the resurrection, he wrote a treatise entitled *An Examination of the Testimony of the Four Evangelists by the Rules of Evidence Administered in Courts of Justice*, (1846). In it he wrote,

> Propagating this new faith, even in the most inoffensive and peaceful manner, they could expect nothing but contempt, stripes, imprisonments, torments and cruel death.... They had every possible motive to review carefully the grounds of their faith, and the evidences of the great facts and truths which they asserted....
> It was therefore impossible that they could have persisted in affirming the truths they have narrated, had not Jesus actually risen from the dead, and had they not known this fact as certainly as they knew any other fact.

Think of it. For the first 300 years of its young life, Christian faith was fiercely persecuted and attacked. Christians commonly had to suffer for their faith, even die for their belief. Every official attempt was made to blot out this young religion, to stamp it from the face of the earth.

During those years, Christian believers and evangelists went about the whole of the Roman Empire telling the story of Jesus' resurrection wherever they went. Those who opposed them would merely have had to prove that their witness was founded on false evidence to end the whole thing. Christianity would have collapsed.

Surely people so determined to deny the truth of Christian faith (of which the resurrection of Christ was the central affirmation) would have, if they could have, denied the historical validity of the message. But there isn't a scrap of evidence that Christian faith was seriously challenged on this score. It would appear quite certain that the people of the time accepted the fact that Jesus of Nazareth had been raised from the dead! The interpretation and implication they might reject, but the fact they could not.

THE WITNESS OF SCRIPTURE

At one point in my faith development and theological training, I found it very difficult to accept the resurrection as historical fact. I tended to believe that it was the result of some kind of mass hysteria.

And yet the more I studied the scriptures, the more I found myself overpowered by the evidence there. The more I questioned the scriptural witness, the more difficulty I found denying its validity. Two things stood out.

For one, the resurrection was not expected.

Remember Thomas, traditionally called "doubting Thomas?"— "If I could see the prints of the nails in His hands and thrust my hand into His side, I still wouldn't believe it!" It was going to take a lot to convince Thomas (John 20:24f).

From the very first, it's evident that His followers were *not* expecting it! The women going to the tomb in the early morning following the Sabbath, finding the stone rolled away, didn't immediately start to jump up and down shouting, "Hallelujah! Christ is risen!" Even when the angel said to them, "He is not here. He is risen!" they were still perplexed and couldn't understand.

They went back and told the others, the men, who only scoffed at them. "Their words seemed to them as idle tales and they didn't believe them" (Luke 24:11). The men thought they were just a bunch of silly women.

When Peter and John ran to the tomb and saw the stone rolled away, and the bandages which had wrapped the body lying there, they still didn't know what to make of it, and went away wondering whether thieves had broken into the tomb and stolen the body—or for some reason the authorities had the soldiers come and take the body away (John 20:1-10).

Remember Mary in the garden? After the other women had left, Mary evidently stayed in the garden, perhaps looking for where the body might have been hidden. She came upon someone she took to be the gardener and said to Him, "Sir, if you have taken Him away, please tell me where you have laid Him?" It was only when Jesus called her by name that she knew Him. "Mary!" He said. "*Rabonni!*" she cried ("Teacher!").

Finally, Jesus Himself appeared among the twelve where they were locked in an upper room with the windows and doors shut and barred. He stood before them and said, "It's not a spirit. Handle me and see. It is I!" And then comes what must be one of the most priceless verses in all scripture—"They believed not yet for joy" (Luke 24:41 AV). They still thought it was *too good to be true*.

Second, if you go back and read the New Testament witness again, you will realize another surprising thing. Not only was He not expected, He was also not particularly welcomed! He was hardly wanted.

The disciples were not overjoyed by His appearing, at least not at first. They were overawed. They were disturbed, profoundly disturbed. All four Gospels use words like "terrified" and "dumbfounded."

The disciples had already begun to adjust to His death, to accept it, to make their own plans for the future. It had been a great dream, quite an experience really—the crowds, the excitement, the healings. They had thought He might be the Messiah, the One who should deliver Israel. But after all, they weren't the first to be mistaken, to be disappointed. Now they had to get back to reality and settle down to what they knew best. They had families to think about. "I'm going fishing," said Simon Peter. "We'll go with you," replied the others (John 21:3).

But then they were suddenly jolted into a new and terrifying existence, and their lives could never, ever be the same again. They were witnesses of the resurrection. Ahead of them now lay new paths, unknown destinations, and journeys into far countries they had never dreamed of undertaking. Ahead of them were threats and persecution, suffering and probable death. With deep instinct, they recognized that everything had changed. No wonder they didn't welcome Him with open arms.

My conclusion then, and now, is that with all the difference in details, there is a central core of reality in the witness of the New Testament that cannot be denied!

THE WITNESS OF HIS SPIRIT IN OUR LIVES!

The third area of evidence to the reality of the resurrection is more esoteric, and yet, to me, the most real of all. It is the witness of the Spirit of God in our hearts, the living presence of Christ.

There is something in us, in our hearts and minds and in our very bones, that says "Yes!" to the good news of God's love, something that affirms the goodness of the Creator, something that wants to believe that God is gracious! There is something in us that recognizes the reality of that life-giving, healing, saving Spirit to which we turn in our need, on whom we call in prayer.

> There has always been a good deal of controversy over the resurrection of Jesus. There has been little over the fact of His being alive in the world. It is as though two men should meet at noonday and begin to argue whether the sun had risen that morning, and after exhausting a great deal of dialectic and rhetoric, one of them suddenly should look up and say, "Why there it is!"[153]

True. Yet I believe that many people hold back today from professing faith in Christ precisely because they feel they lack the sense of the reality of His living Presence. They hear others talk about being "born again," and a new "personal relationship with Jesus," and they feel excluded because they can profess nothing so dramatic, so vivid.

Beware that you do not equate the Spirit of God with a *feeling* of God's presence, especially a good feeling. This "good," exalted feeling is one that is divorced from the reality of the suffering and death of Jesus our Lord. As Bishop Gore said, "The Spirit is not a substitute in the absence of Jesus, but the vehicle of His presence."[154]

---

[153] Willard Brewing, "The Ever-rising Christ," in *Faith For These Times*, Collins, Toronto & New York, 1945, p 133

[154] Quoted by Reginald Fuller in *Interpretation: A Journal of Bible and Theology*, Publishers: Union Theological Seminary in Virginia, Richmond, Virginia, Vol. XXXII,

When I speak of the witness of the Spirit in our hearts and lives, I mean it in the sense that Paul speaks of in Romans 8,

When we cry, "Abba, Father!" it is the Spirit bearing witness with our spirit that we are children of God, and if children, then heirs, heirs of God and fellow heirs with Christ, provided we suffer with Him in order that we may also be glorified with Him (Romans 8:16-17).

In other words, when something within us affirms the ultimate righteousness of life and that at the centre of the universe beats the heart of a loving Father, we may know that it is God's Spirit within us affirming the truth of the living, loving God and Father of our Lord Jesus Christ.

Dr. Sid Gilchrist, a medical missionary in Angola, Africa, in the mid-twentieth century, would tell of the response of Africans when they first heard the Gospel, the proclamation that God is like a loving father. Jumping up and down in delight and happiness, they would exclaim with great excitement, "Yes, that's what God is like! That's what God *must* be like! I knew it all the time."

Something in them prompted them to say, "Yes!"

Something in me, and something in us, prompts us to respond, "Yes! That's what God is like. That's what God *must* be like!"

Therefore we cry, "Abba."

"This Jesus God raised up, and of that we all are witnesses" (Acts 2:32).

WITH WHAT KIND OF BODY DID HE COME?[155]

"I tell you truly that unless a grain of wheat falls into the earth and dies, it remains a single grain; but if it dies, it brings a great harvest" (John 12:24).

I admitted above that I had a difficult time coming to terms with Jesus' resurrection. Even into the second year of my theological studies, preparing to be a preacher, I was inclined to dismiss the accounts as a manifestation of mass hysteria

---

No. 2, April, 1978, p. 183, where he warns against a "Unitarianism of the third Person" of the Trinity.

[155] Thoughts found also in Alan Reynolds, *Reading the Bible for the Love of God*, pp. 71-73.

Then (I think it was the end of my second year), we were given an assignment in our New Testament course to study the New Testament accounts of Jesus' resurrection. I found the witness of those ancient disciples difficult to deny.

For one thing, I found a reality in them that smacks of firsthand experience. They were "witnesses." They don't present an argument, they just tell of what they know, what they saw, touched, and heard. The various discrepancies only add to the reality. They didn't try to hide them. They just "told it as they saw it.'

As I've said, it was obvious they didn't expect it. They didn't welcome him. They were surprised. Moreover, they were frightened, even terrified. They themselves were slow, exceedingly slow, to be convinced. The women came back from the tomb, Peter and John had gone to inspect the tomb, Mary had encountered Him in the garden, and then the two travellers returned to Jerusalem from Emmaus with their witness. Then Jesus Himself appeared to them, and showed them His hands and His feet. Recall again that amazing verse, "They believed not yet for joy." They still didn't believe because it was just too good to be true.

"If Christ was not raised," wrote Paul, "then our Gospel is null and void, and so is your faith, and we turn out to be lying witness for God... If it is for this life only that Christ has given us hope, we of all people are most to be pitied! But the truth is that Christ *has* been raised to life" (I Corinthians 15:14-19).

It was this conviction that sent those early believers charging into the world of their time like newsboys with an extra edition, "Read all about it: Man raised from the dead!" With my modern dose of scepticism, I asked for evidence that would satisfy my contemporary understanding of the working of the universe. I asked "What actually happened?" Gradually I realized that this was it. This is what actually happened.

Paul foresaw the questioners, people like us who would ask, "How are the dead raised? With what kind of body to they come?" (I Corinthians 15:35). The people two thousand years ago were not naive. They knew that when a body was put into the ground, it decayed and turned back to dust.

And with what kind of body, specifically, did Jesus come? The being that appeared to the disciples was not some vaporous spirit, but rather a visible presence, a "body" of some sort with some kind of objective reality. But it was also and quite obviously not simply a "physical body," at least in the sense we commonly use the word "physical."

I find myself frustrated by the arguments whether Jesus' resurrection was physical or spiritual. Some people assert that it was "only spiritual." Then others reply that if we do not believe in "a literal physical resurrection," our faith is vain and our Gospel null and void.

I suggest to you that such argumentation is vain, the issue being null and void. We simply cannot comprehend the reality of what happened by the words "spiritual" and "physical," as we tend to use them and understand them today. In some ways, the people of that time, not constrained by the Cartesian dualism of the physical and the spiritual, had better understanding than we do.

NOT MERELY SPIRITUAL

On the one hand, I don't think we can speak of His resurrection as merely spiritual.

It wasn't a vague awareness of a spiritual presence that dawned gradually upon them. It was something that hit them unexpectedly, like a bolt out of the blue. It was Jesus who appeared to them. It was really Him. And it changed the whole course of their thinking, their expectations, and their very lives.

"Handle me and see," He said to them. It's as though Luke wants to drive home to us the fact that it was not merely spiritual, as though he says, "I want you to understand there can be no mistake about it." Jesus, says Luke, appeared to all the disciples and invited them to touch Him—no, not just touch, to "handle." He wanted them to know for sure that He was not just a spirit. "Handle me and see," He said, "a spirit does not have flesh and bones as I have." And to make it completely sure, Luke tells us that He took a piece of broiled fish and ate before them (Luke 24:36-43).

In John's Gospel, too (John 21:9-14), He prepares breakfast for them on the shore of the Sea of Galilee, and it's in John's Gospel (John 20:19-29) that He invited Thomas, "doubting Thomas," to thrust his finger into the nail prints in His hands and thrust his hands into the hole in His side (John 20:26-28).

It's evident that these evangelists, in spite of all the discrepancies of the various narratives, were trying very hard to say that it was not merely a spiritual apparition. It was really Jesus who had been crucified, Jesus whom they had known in the flesh, whom they had seen and touched and with whom they had so many times broken bread. It was really Jesus who appeared to them.

NOT SIMPLY PHYSICAL

Yet, if His resurrection was not merely spiritual, it was also not "simply physical."

The bandages in which the body had been wrapped were lying, we are told, undisturbed (John 20:6-7)—as though the body had somehow passed through them.

He seemed able to appear and disappear in a very strange manner. He could appear before them in a room with the doors and windows shut and barred.

Perhaps even stranger, those who had known Him so well in the flesh didn't always recognize Him in His resurrected body. Mary, in the garden, mistook Him for the gardener (John 20:11-18), and it doesn't satisfy me to claim that it was because of the dimness of the early morning light. The two "followers" on the road to Emmaus walked with Him and talked with Him and yet didn't recognize Him until "He was made known to them in the breaking of bread" (Luke 24:13-32).

Whatever this "body" was, it seems obvious that it was not simply a physical resurrection. It was not the resuscitation of a corpse, a dead body come back to life. It was something more.

If it had been simply a physical resuscitation and no more, it seems reasonable to suppose that there would have been simply the resumption of their former relationship, a return to what had been before. But it was obviously something very different. He was no longer to them just "Rabbi," their teacher and spiritual leader. Now they fell down before Him and called Him "Lord," the Hebrew term signifying the actual person of God. Thomas, who had been so full of doubt, fell to his knees and cried, "My Lord and my God."

WHAT IS THE "PHYSICAL?"

What is the "physical," in any case? It was Rene Descartes, credited as the father of modern philosophy and the scientific method, who made the clear distinction between "physical substance" and "spiritual substance." He was never too clear about what he meant by "spiritual substance," but "physical substance" was that which we can see, taste, smell, or knock against. It was, he believed, made up of tiny material particles that he called "atoms," by which he meant the smallest and indivisible particles of matter (from the Greek *atomos*, meaning "indivisible.")

But, in this century, we have divided the atom. We no longer understand it as a tiny indivisible particle of matter. Physicists speak of a whole world of sub-atomic particles. We tend rather to understand physical matter as a form of energy.

In 1905, Albert Einstein introduced the seemingly simple formula $E=mc^2$—energy equals mass times the speed of light squared. It changed the way we understand the world around us.

Mass, matter, physical substance is a form of energy. The building around you, the chair on which you are sitting, the flesh and bones that give us substance, these we say are forms, concentrations of energy. Is energy physical, or spiritual? The traditional terms no longer apply.

The body in which Jesus rose from the dead—was it physical, or spiritual? That body that passed through the wrappings of the grave, which He told Mary not to touch, which walked with them on the road to Emmaus and which appeared in the upper room and on the shores of Galilee—was it physical, or spiritual?

THE "SPIRITUAL BODY"

"What foolish questions!" wrote Paul.

> *The seed you sow does not come to life unless it has first died!. And what you sow is not the body that shall be, but a bare grain— of wheat, or something else. But God gives it the body of His choice, each seed its own particular body....*
>
> *So it is with the resurrection of the dead. When the body is buried it is mortal. When it is raised, it is immortal. When buried, it is ugly and weak. When raised, it is beautiful and strong. It is buried a physical body, but when it is raised it will be a spiritual body* (I Cor. 15:35-38, 42-44).

As there is a "physical body," says Paul, so there is a "spiritual body." The physical body is finally put in the ground to die, like a kernel of wheat. "These mortal bodies of ours are not fit to live forever." But like the kernel of wheat, the physical body, in dying, may bring forth a far more glorious creation than could ever be imagined by looking at the seed.

Remember Jesus' words about having "faith as a grain of mustard seed" (Matthew 17:20). The mustard seed is very small, only a speck of a thing, the tiniest of seeds. Yet from it grows one of the largest plants of Palestine, so large that the birds of the air come to roost in its branches (Matthew 13:31-32).

"Lo," said Paul, "I show you a mystery." The body in which Jesus rose is still a mystery to us, perhaps not answerable in our present understanding. It does seem certain, however, that it was neither merely spiritual, nor simply physical. He came to them in a new body, the old body consumed. The new body was raised from the dead, and was a glorious body unlike the old, as the flower from the seed, the butterfly from the cocoon, or the oak from the acorn.

The Heart's True Home!

THIS WORLD IS NOT MY HOME

One hundred years ago, Christianity was accused of being too other-worldly, so heavenly minded that it was of no earthly use. Karl Marx could speak of religion as "the opiate of the people," and his followers would sing the taunt,

> Work and pray, live on hay,
> You'll get pie in the sky when you die.[156]

Of course, for most people life was hard labour and small reward, and often disease or accident made it dangerous and short. For people like the African slaves of America, hope was beyond this life, and life's greatest joy consisted in looking forward to goin' over Jordan. "This world is not my home, I'm only passin' through."

Our Christianity today, however, tends to be very this-worldly. Sermons focus on present world problems, the struggle

---

[156] Attributed to Joe Hill (Joseph Hillstom), labour organizer for the Industrial Workers of the World (I.W.W.) Hill, something of an anarchist, was executed in 1915 on a disputed murder charge.

for justice and peace, or how to find peace of mind or spiritual and material success! We seldom hear a sermon on heaven and the hope of immortality.

Yet, even in the midst of our relative comfort and security, we never seem to be perfectly content. There is, it seems, a sense in which this life in itself is never complete for us. Life, I say, points beyond itself for its fulfillment, and our present world (glorious as it may be) and this life (good as it so often is), is never enough. We are forced to seek our ultimate fulfillment beyond this life.

> For men are homesick in their homes,
> And strangers under the sun,
> And they lay their heads in a foreign land
> Whenever the day is done.[157]

"The heart's true home" is no place in this world. It's in that place Jesus said, "In my Father's house are many rooms" (John 14:2 RSV). This is not simply an egocentric desire for individual immortality; it's part of being "created in the image of God." God "has placed eternity in our hearts" (Ecclesiastes 3:10).

> *The fundamental fact of human existence is that this trust in God, this faith, is the firm foundation under everything that makes life worth living. It's our handle on what we can't see. The act of faith is what distinguished people of God in days of old, set them above the crowd. ... They died without receiving all that God had promised them, but they saw it in the distance and were glad.*

> *They knew that this earth was not their real home and that they were just transients here, sojourners. It's obvious, by their lives, that they were looking forward to their real home in heaven. If they had wanted to, they could have gone back to their old country. But they were after a far better country than that, their true home in heaven.*

> (From Hebrews 11, *The Message*—a translation of the New Testament by Eugene Peterson.)

---

[157] G. K. Chesterton, "The House of Christmas," in *Masterpieces of Religious Verse*, ed. James Dalton Morrison, Harper & Brothers Publishers, New York and London, 1948, No.504, p. 162.

Again, remember the words of Augustine: "Thou hast made us for Thyself, and our hearts are restless till they find their rest in Thee." We are created for eternity, and "our hearts are restless" until they find rest in that which God has prepared for us.

A SPIRITUAL STATE, NOT A PHYSICAL PLACE

Traditionally, we have tended to think of heaven in physical imagery—our home "beyond the sky," with pearly gates, golden streets, angels with harps, and a great white throne. This comes, in part, from the Book of Revelation with its powerful, poetic imagery. But it is *poetic* imagery, not physical description.

This imagery tends to be lacking in strength today. Astronauts, circling the earth in space, have seen no pearly gates, and most of our "young people" would rather play a computer game or go to a movie than play a harp. In an affluent age, pearls and gold and other precious stones don't seem so special or remote, and certainly far from ethereal.

Of course, only very small children and those with the minds of very small children believe that the streets of heaven are literally and physically "paved with pure gold." We are attempting to describe something that is basically indescribable, to put into words something that really can't be put into words. Even if we did know exactly what heaven is like, we still couldn't describe it.

But some things can be said.

Heaven is not a place "up there," somewhere "way beyond the blue." Recent astronomical speculation is that the centre of the universe is some 28,000 light years from us. A light year is roughly 63,000 times the distance of the earth from the sun (or about six million million miles). The farthest stars of the universe are thought to be some two billion light years away. Think of it. How fast and far does a soul have to go to get to heaven? How long will it take? These are the kinds of ridiculous questions that are inevitable if we try to take this kind of imagery as literal physical fact.

When we talk about heaven, we're not talking about a physical place, at least not in spatial terms. It's not "up there" or "out there!" No matter how far our spaceships or our radio scopes may reach, they will never find heaven. Heaven is a spiritual state, not a physical place. It is a condition, not a position.

Spirit, of course, doesn't occupy space. By definition, spirit is that which doesn't have dimension or weight or position. It is outside the dimensions of space. It's another dimension entirely. That's why it's senseless to speak of heaven as being overcrowded with the accumulation of souls through the ages, as though heaven is a kind of theatre with a limited seating capacity.

THAT CLOSE TO HOME

As heaven is a spiritual state rather than a physical place, it may be much closer to us than we have realized. For instance, "going to heaven" is more a matter of being transformed (or as the Bible says, "translated") than it is being transported.

Don't we have glimpses of heaven right here and now—as when two people love each other, or in the glow of a mother's eyes as she looks at her newborn child? When the family is gathered around the table, and it's one of those good times full of joy and love, isn't that a little bit like heaven?

There's an incident in an old Laurel and Hardy movie called "Two Yanks in London." It's a story of two American soldiers in London during World War I. They're looking at a map of the world. They find London, then they find New York, and finally one turns to the other and holds up his fingers, saying, "Why, we're just that far from home!"

THE "SPIRITUAL BODY"

The Biblical tradition affirmed "the resurrection of the body." The classical (Greek and Roman) tradition believed in "the immortality of the soul." Most of us probably think more in terms of the immortality of the soul than the resurrection of the body, but the New Testament affirms the resurrection of the body.

The common understanding was that "the soul" was a spark of divinity within us, a drop of immortality which, when we die, falls back into the ocean of infinity, the spark back into the great infinite fire. Our speck of consciousness becomes again a part of the great cosmic consciousness of the universe.

But the New Testament seems to affirm that after death we can still claim a self-conscious existence. This is how I understand the phrase "the resurrection of the body." What is raised is not some part of us called "the soul" that is reabsorbed into spiritual infinity. Rather, it is *you*. *You*, as a self-conscious being, are brought to the fulfillment that God has planned for you from the beginning. Surely this is part of what it means to say that we are "created in God's image."

We are changed, yes. No doubt of it. It's not just a remoulding of the molecules of our physical bodies so that we go on interminably with all the aches and pains we've known here—no more than the resurrection body of Jesus was simply a resuscitation of his physical body. We are transformed into a new and glorious body, what Paul calls "a spiritual body." He says, "It is sown a physical (natural) body. It is raised a spiritual body. If there is a physical body, there is also a spiritual body" (I Corinthians 15:44).

Is this so strange? Think for a minute of the changes that have taken place in your physical body during your lifetime. You started out a mulling, puking infant, became a gawky teenager, gained physical maturity, put on weight, and then perhaps began to lose hair and teeth. Some of us have changed quite a bit over the course of years, even those with only a couple dozen years to count. And yet, you know yourself still to be yourself. You know that you're the same person that you were half-a-lifetime ago or more.

So when this final great change comes, I believe that we will still know ourselves to be ourselves. We will still be self-conscious identities.

NOT WHAT YOU LOOK LIKE, BUT WHO YOU ARE

If we are self-conscious beings, if we are "spiritual bodies," will we know each other? And if so, how will we know each other? When I think of other people, I think of their physical features. If I try to think of them apart from their physical features, I can't really think of them at all. It seems that I can't think of others as pure spirit.

This bothered me for a long time, until I realized that when I thought of those who were nearest and dearest to me, I didn't think of what they looked like, but *who they were*. When I remember my mother, I don't think of her physical appearance. It's something else, but I know it's her. And when I think of myself, I don't think of what I look like but who I am.

The "soul," in the Biblical sense, is not some vague spiritual entity. The soul is you. *You don't have a soul, you are a soul.*

YOUR ROOM—IN THE FATHER'S HOUSE

Jesus, on that last night of His life on earth, the night on which he was betrayed, gathered with His disciples in the Upper Room for the meal we call "the last supper." According to the Gospel of John, he said to them the words that we remember and cherish two thousand years later:

> *Let not your hearts be troubled. You believe in God? Then trust in me... In my Father's house are many rooms... I go to prepare yours for you* (John 14:1-2, my paraphrase).

It's a beautiful passage, but it didn't make much sense to me until I realized its intended meaning. When I was a child, in my own home, my father's house, I had my own room. It wasn't very big, or very elegant. It had a curtain instead of a door, and a shelf with a curtain around it for a closet. It had blue wallpaper that I liked very much.

When I think of that room, I get a certain feeling. It represents for me the comfort and security that love gives. There I knew and felt the love and the security that my mother and my father brought to my life. I'm very grateful for that memory (though many do not have such fond memories of their father's house).

Do you see what Jesus was saying? This is your room, in your heavenly Father's house. And "I go to get it ready for you."

The thing that made your childhood house into a home was the love that you knew and received there, the love of your mother and father. It is the love of our God, whom Jesus called "Father," which makes God's house (which we call heaven) *our heart's true home.*

CHAPTER 7

WHO JESUS IS

"Everybody ought to know ... who Jesus is"[158]

Who Do You Say?

It was six men of Indostan,
To learning much inclined,
Who went to see the elephant
(Though all of them were blind),
That each by observation
Might satisfy his mind.

The first approached the elephant
And, happening to fall
Against his broad and sturdy side,
At once began to bawl:
"God bless me but the elephant
Is nothing but a wall!"

The second, feeling the tusk,
"so round and smooth and sharp,"
concluded the elephant was a spear.
The third, ... happening to take
The squirming trunk within his hands,
concluded the elephant was a snake.

The fourth, feeling about the elephant's knee,
took the elephant for a tree.
The fifth thought the ear was a fan,

---

[158] Folk song of the 20th century.

and the sixth, feeling the tail,
took the elephant for a rope.

And so these men of Indostan
Disputed loud and long,
Each in his own opinion
Exceeding stiff and strong,
Though each was partly in the right
And all were in the wrong.[159]

This poem has been used to illustrate the vastness of the reality of God, how little we know of the totality. It's also true of the way so many have seen and understood Jesus Christ from various perspectives.

Some have seen Jesus as a great ethical teacher who taught people how to live with one another. Others have called Jesus "the great Physician," healing the lame and the blind. Others have seen Jesus as a mystic-religious leader, founder of one of the world's great religions. Others have seen Jesus as "the Saviour," who forgives our sins and grants believers everlasting life.

Yes, the story of the blind men and the elephant has a certain truth and relevance. But we shouldn't overlook the fact that *none of these men recognized the elephant as an elephant*!

At a crucial point in His ministry, Jesus led His closest followers, the twelve disciples, north into the Gentile territory today called Banias, then called Caesarea Phillippi. It was for them a time of "retreat," of quietness and reflection. There, where the waters of the Jordan River come gushing, fresh and cold, from the southern slope of Mount Hermon, Jesus taught and talked with this inner circle of his followers.[160]

"Who do people say that I am?" He asked them. The belief of the time allowed for the "return" of some of the historical leaders of the people's past. His disciples reported the various rumours and opinions circulating the hills of Galilee.

---

[159] John Godfrey Saxe, "The Blind Men and the Elephant," in *Masterpieces of Religious Verse*, ed. James Dalton Morrison, Harper and Brothers Publishers, New York and London, 1948, No. 1412, p. 428.

[160] Of course we cannot be certain of the exact location, but this beautiful spot lies in my memory and I can well imagine that this is the place where Peter's great confession took place.

Some said that He might be Elijah, the fiery prophet who didn't hesitate to confront the king himself and to call him to account for the injustice he had committed (I Kings 17f). This could well have been the comment of the scribes and Pharisees, to whom He most often showed His anger, accusing them of self-righteousness and hypocrisy. The qualities Jesus most condemned, remember, were self-righteousness and hypocrisy.

Some said he was John the Baptist. Herod, no doubt, for one. It was Herod who said of Jesus, "It is John, whom I slew, risen from the dead!" In his guilt, Herod had respected John, even feared him. That's why, when John openly condemned Herod for marrying his brother's wife, Herod had John imprisoned. Later, when young Salome danced and Herod made his foolish promise to give her anything she asked, up to half his kingdom, she requested "the head of John the Baptist on a platter." Herod had been forced to give the order to have John beheaded, and had watched as the head of John the Baptist was brought to her. Perhaps in his dreams, Herod still saw that great bloody head on its silver platter (note Mark 6:14-29).

Others said he was Jeremiah, the great-hearted prophet who wept tears of anguish over the hard-hearted and stiff-necked people who would not hear his words nor heed the warning God had given him to say to them.

Like the blind men and the elephant, people saw Jesus in different ways, according to their own experience of Him.

But then Jesus turned to the disciples, this little group who had been with him through it all, and asked them, not what other people were saying, but "Who do you say that I am?"

You can imagine the pause, the silence, the "moment of truth." You may, perhaps, hear the question now, directed to you. We all face the same question. What do *we* make of Jesus?

It was Simon Peter, often the spokesman of the group, who answered: *"You are the Messiah!"*

In the Hebrew, it's "Messiah." In the Greek, it's "Christ." The meaning is the same—God's anointed, God's Promised One, who would deliver the people from oppression and all injustice, rule with righteousness and strength, and bring "a perfect and permanent kingdom characterized by peace and prosperity, righteousness, justice, and the knowledge and true worship of

God."[161] While others saw Jesus as many things, it was the disciples who saw Him as the Messiah, the Promised One, God's great affirmation for humanity.

For us who call ourselves "Christians," what does it mean to call Jesus "Christ?" After all, it's not a proper name. It's a title.

I hope there will be some who read this who will come to see and understand Jesus not simply as a great human being and religious teacher, one who lived long ago and whose teachings we try to follow, but also know Him as the fulfillment of what God calls us in our humanity to be and do. In that very humanity, Jesus presents to us the very character and Person of God.

Let me warn you, though, that to see and know Jesus Christ in this way will mean that your life will be changed. You may never again call your life your own or look on your possessions as yours, to use for your own pleasure regardless of the needs of others. You may not again see life as something to be lived for your own benefit apart from the happiness of others, especially those who are poor, weak, or oppressed.

But also, you may never again see life as meaningless and empty, without purpose or the possibility of fulfillment. You may forever know the presence of the One who against all odds gives comfort and hope.

So, let us reflect on the question He asked His disciples that day long ago on the grassy slopes of Mount Hermon. Who do you say Jesus is? Today, sitting where you are, reading this, who do you say Jesus is?

Like the blind men and the elephant, do you see just a part here and a bit there? Or do you say, with Peter and the others, "Here is the One God intended for us, that we should know what we are to be and know that God is for us and with us, in Spirit and in Truth."

Strangely, you may find:

He comes to us, as He came to them. He offers to us the inestimable privilege He offered to them. We may be His people. He will begin with us where we are, as He began with them, not expecting more than we can do or be, but asking for our loyalty, our love, our obedience. Then He can set us to the tasks He has

---

[161] *Interpreter's Dictionary of the Bible*, Vol. I, p. 563.

for us. We too shall enter that transforming friendship and do His
blessed will, and in that glorious doing find the meaning of life.[162]

God Was in Christ

The doctrine of the incarnation is essential to the fabric of the
Christian faith. Remove or deny this insight, and the Christian
faith, like a knitted garment, begins to unravel, lose its shape, and
become of no significance.[163]

"Incarnation" means *to enflesh*. Christian faith claims that the One
we call "Jesus Christ" is "God enfleshed," that in Him God is
present as a human being. This is a stupendous assertion, and we
shouldn't make it without some thought, some basis, some
understanding that has meaning for us. The statement sounds
paradoxical, the two realities seem to be self-contradictory. It is
the assertion that theologians Karl Barth and Reinhold Niebuhr
have both called "the impossible possibility." How can anyone be
both "man" and "God?" At Christmas, we sing about the baby in
the manger, "veiled in flesh the Godhead see." If you claim to
believe it, do you sometimes stop to think about what it means?
How do you explain it to others, to your children for instance?

Orthodox Christian doctrine, as developed by the great church
Councils of the fourth century and expressed in the traditional
creeds of the church, has claimed that Jesus is *both* "fully human
and fully divine." How can we say of anyone, any human being?
How can anyone be both fully human and fully divine?

At the same time, we must recognize that this belief seems to
be the very essence of the message of the New Testament. It is
very difficult to deny this article of faith in the light of the New
Testament witnesses. The disciples, though they were not scholars,
were not fools.

---

[162] Leslie Weatherhead, *It Happened In Palestine*, Hodder and Stoughton, London, 1936, p.
40.
[163] Alister McGrath, *Understanding Doctrine: Its Purpose and Relevance for Today*,
Hodder & Stoughton, London, 1990, pp. 176-178.

They probably had as much intelligence as you or me, perhaps more. Not only that, they were all strict Jews, pledged to fight idolatry, pledged to defend monotheism to the death. For such men to call Jesus Lord is indeed startling.[164]

They were not quick to reach this conclusion. It was obviously very difficult for them. But it seemed the only way they could understand what had happened, the only way they could make sense of it.

This supreme mystery of Christian faith is not only proclaimed implicitly throughout the New Testament but is also proclaimed explicitly in a number of specific instances. "He is the very image of the invisible God... In Him the fullness of God was pleased to dwell" (Colossians 2:9). "Without doubt, the mystery of our religion is great: God was revealed in flesh" (I Timothy 3:16, a portion of an early Christian hymn). "He reflects the glory of God and bears the very stamp of God's nature" (Hebrews 1:3).

One significant passage (called "the *kenosis* passage," from the Greek word meaning "emptying"), is found at Philippians 2:5-11.[165] Though there can be no certain date, the *Interpreter's Dictionary of the Bible*[166] dates the Philippian letter little more than twenty years after Jesus' death (54-55AD) and this passage appears to be a Christian hymn predating the letter to the church at Philippi and reaching into the very early life of the Christian community.

It claims that "Christ Jesus" had always been part of God, sharing the glory of God, but "emptied" Himself of all that glory, thought it not something to be clutched or held onto, and was born a human being, a man, lived the life of a servant, and submitted even to human death, and "the death He died was that of a common criminal."[167]

---

[164] Donald Mathers, *The Word and the Way*, The United Church Publishing House, Toronto, 1962, p. 122.

[165] Note D. M. Baillie, *God Was In Christ: An Essay On The Incarnation And Atonement*, Faber and Faber Ltd., London, 1948, pp. 94-98. The old book is still one of the best discussions of the Incarnation.

[166] *Interpreter's Dictionary of the Bible*, Vol.. 4, p. 790.

[167] J. B. Phillips, *The New Testament In Modern English*, Geoffrey Bles, London, 1960, Philippians 2:8.

There are some who bemoan the complex theological and intricate creedal statements of the church tradition, who prefer what they call "the simple teachings of Jesus," but one cannot divorce the teaching from the life, the doctrine from the person.

For instance, part of Jesus' teaching is the story of the shepherd who leaves his flock of ninety-nine sheep and goes into the mountains to look for one lost sheep. Isn't Jesus saying, "God is like that," like the good shepherd who will go to any length to save the lost ones of his fold—even to taking on their flesh and living as one of them? And isn't that the very Spirit we see in Jesus Himself, One who would go to any length, even a cross, to show us the meaning of life and love?

Claude Montefiore, a Jewish scholar who set himself to see if there was anything new and distinctive in Jesus' teaching, singled out the picture of the shepherd going into the wilderness to seek a lost sheep, and described it as "the picture of God as not merely receiving those who turn to Him, but as taking the initiative in seeking those who have not turned to Him."[168] Here is the distinctive message of the New Testament, embodied in Jesus— the God who goes out to seek the lost sheep, the woman who turns the house upside down to find the lost coin.

This God does not sit in heaven waiting for us to come to Him, but rather comes to us, submitting to human hatred, suffering, and even death. This is the God who was in Christ.

Our time, however, asks for "the facts." Both the New Testament and all those complex statements of the early church were attempts to understand the facts of the life, teachings, amazing power, death, and resurrection of this same Jesus. They were not the fruit of credulous and simple-minded people, or of ancient scholars fighting over non-essential points of doctrine. They were attempts to understand, to comprehend, and to express their understanding in as systematic and reasonable way as possible.

---

[168] Baillie, *God Was In Christ*, p. 63 (see note 165).

The Incarnation is not an added difficulty (to Christian understanding) but is rather the sole way in which the Christian conception of God becomes credible or even expressible.[169]

The seeming impossibility of this belief appears to be a problem for many people today, but we must also face the fact that it seems absolutely necessary if we are to make sense of the reality of Jesus Christ as presented to us in the New Testament.

How then are we to understand?

The phrase I've developed to "say it for me" is this:

In Jesus, whom we call Christ,
we see the fulfillment of humanity
and the essence of divinity.

THE FULFILLMENT OF HUMANITY

It may seem obvious to say that Jesus was a human being—but stop a minute and think about it. On the one hand, we have so commonly deified the man that what emerges is something both more than and less than human.

We make Jesus more than human when we imagine that he has powers beyond any human ability, knowledge that we cannot have. We may think that we are magnifying the reality of the Incarnation when we bestow upon the historical figure of Jesus powers and knowledge that are impossible to any creature of flesh living in space and time, but we are in fact denying the full humanity of the One we call Lord. We may think we are magnifying our Lord, but we are in fact denying His humanity.

We make Jesus less than human when we deny to our understanding of Jesus the full reality of our humanity. Certainly the scripture tells us that "Jesus wept" (John 11:35), and that he was at times hungry and thirsty (e.g. John 4:7). But when we think of Jesus, we don't like to think of things like human sweat and smelly feet and the ordinary functions of human defecation. We pretty up the stable and the manger for the Christmas pageant but the place was no doubt pretty dirty and smelly, and no doubt the baby dirtied his diapers as any baby would. When he prayed in Gethsemane, those tears and sweat falling as "great drops of

---

[169] ibid., 65.

blood," were those tears and sweat only sham? Standing in the shadow of the cross, did he have a calm assurance that all would be well?

The reality of Jesus as a human being is very meaningful for me, for two reasons.

The first is that, as a human being, I can feel an identity with Him. As a human being, He knows what I feel, knows what I experience. Pain and suffering and death he knew, and also the ordinary daily struggle that life can be. He "identifies" with me, and so I can identify with Him. He was "flesh" as we are flesh, male and female. He was "mortal" as we are mortal, and died as we all must die.

The other reason Jesus' humanity is important for me is that I see in Jesus an "ideal"—a humanity beyond what I am, and which calls me to be more than I am. I see in Him the fulfillment of what I would hope to be in my own humanity. That's why I can say I "worship" Him, because I do believe that not only was He human, as I am human, but that He is the fulfillment of our humanity, of all that we are called and purposed to be. This fulfillment we find in that quality of self-giving love (*agape*), the most human of all human qualities, and the most divine.

I see both of these realities intended in that phrase which He so often used, according to the Gospels, traditionally translated "the Son of Man." "Who do people say that the Son of Man is?" He asked His disciples. And went on to tell them, "the Son of Man must suffer ... and be crucified" (Mark 8:27f). But later He said to them, "You shall see the Son of Man coming in His glory with all the holy angels" (Matthew 25:31).

It seems He used the term in two ways. In one way, He used it in reference to His identification with our human condition: "The Son of Man must suffer many things." In another way, He used it in the sense of His own fulfilment: "The Son of Man must come again in glory and all the holy angels with Him." It appears to be both a reference to His humanity and the sense in which He was the fulfillment of humanity, what humanity is meant to be or to become.

He seemed to use it not only in reference to Himself, but sometimes as though it referred to a group of people: a collective humanity, a redeemed humanity, a "righteous remnant" (more about this in a moment), the people of the divine community of the reign of God, the *qe'hal ethonai*, the "people of God."

These understandings reflect meanings found in the Old Testament. The prophet Ezekiel used the term to refer to himself, to his own humanity. Or rather, it was God's form of address to the prophet. It seemed a reminder of his mortality in spite of his prophetic office. "The Human One" would not be a bad translation, one who is, as we might say, a "mere mortal."

But the phrase was used in the Book of Daniel in another way—the One who would come in the last days, in mighty power, to redeem Israel and come out of the sky in clouds of glory with an army of angels. This is more the sense in which the people of Jesus' own day would have come to understand it. Through the literature of what is called "the intertestimental period," the several hundred years immediately before the birth of Jesus,[170] there is the expectation of the "Elect" or "Chosen One," in whom there would be great power and the spirit of wisdom and understanding. He would sit on a throne of glory and judge all people. In that day, righteousness would prevail, and those who were counted as righteous would live in His presence forever.

The phrase " Son of Man" seems to be implicit in the writing of the ones we call "First and Second Isaiah," though it does not appear explicitly. The "First Isaiah," whose writings are found in the first thirty-nine chapters of the Book of Isaiah, spoke of a "righteous remnant" who would persevere and remain faithful to God's purposes through all the sufferings and ambiguities of life.

In the one or ones we call "Second Isaiah" (because the last twenty-six chapters of the book seem to be the product of not just one prophet but several), this "righteous remnant," this "redeemed humanity," seems to be reduced to just one human being, the One called God's "suffering servant," who would passively suffer to redeem and save "the world."

> *Surely He has borne our griefs and carried our sorrows... He was wounded for our transgressions, bruised for our iniquities. Upon Him was laid the punishment that makes us whole, and by His stripes we are healed* (Isaiah 53:4-5).

---

[170] E.g. in "the Similitudes of Enoch," chapters 37-71 of the Book of Enoch.

At the beginning of this chapter, I put to you the question, "Who do you say that Jesus is?" To be fair, I must ask myself what it means to me to speak of Jesus as "the fulfillment of humanity." Who do I say that Jesus is?

What is it that makes us human? What is unique about our humanity?

Philosophers have wrestled with this question at least since Aristotle called human beings "rational animals." We have noted that Augustine spoke of memory as our capacity to transcend time, to remember the past and anticipate the future, so that we must see ourselves as creatures not simply of time but also of eternity (as the Book of Ecclesiastes says, "God has placed eternity in our hearts" Ecclesiastes 3:11).

Two theologians, who have added their perspectives in modern times, are Emil Brunner and Reinhold Niebuhr. Brunner focused on our "response-ability," our ability to respond rather than merely react, and therefore our sense of accountability for what we do (taken to the extreme, we know our ultimate responsibility is to God). Reinhold Niebuhr, as we noted in Chapter 2, spoke in his theology of our human ability of self-transcendence, to see ourselves in the dimensions of space and time, so that we are therefore able to transcend the dimensions of space and time. Therefore we cannot understand ourselves simply in empirical terms.

As we noted, Niebuhr claims further that this ability of self-transcendence is the basis of human freedom. Because we are able to see ourselves, we are able to some extent to change ourselves, or our circumstances. This is why we are "responsible." We are able to "respond" in freedom to others or a given situation, and therefore bear this sense of accountability for what we do.

Niebuhr also says that our ability of self-transcendence is indeterminate. He speaks of "the indeterminate possibilities of the human personality," by which he means that it is theoretically without limit. We can see ourselves sitting in this place at this time, but we can also see ourselves seeing ourselves, and so on. While there are necessary and physical limits to our freedom, it is nevertheless true to say that theoretically our possibilities are limitless.

In other words (or, at least, my words), we trail off, so to speak, into infinity. We realize the Infinite and the Eternal. We feel a sense of responsibility for all that is, a sense of "ultimate responsibility."

I have claimed that the highest expression of our humanity is what the New Testament calls *agape*, the kind of self-giving love which we see in the love of a mother willing to sacrifice herself for her children. This is the word used in the New Testament to define the love of God that we see and know in Jesus our Lord.[171] In the life and ministry of Jesus, in His suffering and death upon the cross, we see the highest expression of this self-giving love.

Do you see how this reflects upon our theme? In Jesus, whom we call Christ, we see the epitome, the fulfillment, of this humanity. We see and know the One who so transcended His own interests that He was able to give Himself in freedom. We see the One who personalized, who incarnated, this *agape*, this Love, who even on the cross could cry, "Father, forgive them." We see and know the One who was what God intended us all to be—the fulfillment of our humanity.

Could this also be "the essence of divinity?"

THE ESSENCE OF DIVINITY

We may acknowledge God as "the Force," the power behind the wind and the wave. We may understand God as "the Mind" behind the law and order of the universe. But what is God like? We may agree with Albert Einstein that God is subtle, but how do we know that God is not malicious?

God as the Power behind the wind and the wave

Conscious of our own existence and of the world around us, we look about us at the forces of creation, at the stormy sea or the mighty mountains, at the beauty and magnificence of life in all its complexity and majesty, and we sense that there must be a Creator.

As a student minister in Saskatchewan, I would sometimes go out at night to look at the stars. There was a hay wagon in the backyard of the farm where I was staying, and I'd lie down on it,

---

[171] For a fuller exposition of the meaning of Christian love, note Reynolds, *Reading the Bible For The Love of God,* chp. 9, especially "The Love God Defines," pp. 127-132.

with my hands under my head, and just stare up at that vast sky with its billions of stars. In British Columbia, where I live now, we have magnificent scenery, but those who have lived on the prairies know that we have nothing to compare to the prairie sky, that great vaulted dome stretching from far horizon to far horizon. Looking up at night into that vast crater, I couldn't help but be conscious of a sense of infinity, a sense of awe at the wonder of the universe, the majesty and magnificence of the Creator.

We look at the overwhelming power of the ocean in a storm, the uncontrollable fury of the hurricane or tornado, the destructiveness of an earthquake or tsunami, and we are conscious of a force so much greater than any human strength. Some people think of God in these terms—"the Force," primarily as the Power behind the wind and the wave.

God as intelligence, "Mind"

But is it enough to think of God simply as physical power?

At this point, I hope you will accept what seems to me to be axiomatic—that *God, if God be God, must be at least as great as the things God has created.* Human beings have achieved many wonderful things, from the wheel to walking on the moon. But we have never created anything as wonderful as ourselves. The invention is never greater than the inventor. The creation is never greater than the Creator.

Surely God must be at least as vast as the universe, as powerful as the volcano. Surely God must be as intelligent as the intelligence He has created.

We have to pass from mere power and realize that when we speak of God we speak also of a certain law and order in creation, of an intelligence, a "Mind," behind it all. This is what filled Albert Einstein with awe, the sense of order and intelligence he could see in all creation. Immanuel Kant wrote, at the conclusion of his *Critique of Practical Reason,*

> Two things fill the mind with ever new and increasing wonder and awe, the more often and the more seriously reflection concentrates upon them: the starry heavens above me and the moral law within me.

God as "Person"

But is it enough to think of God as Power and Mind? How do we know what God is like? How do we know that God is good? How can we know, unless we know God as Person.

We have said that God is greater than the greatest that God has made. What is the greatest thing God has made?

Surely we must say that the greatest thing God has made is not a thing at all. At the risk of being accused of anthropocentricity (the understanding of ourselves which puts humanity at the centre of the universe), I would still maintain that the greatest thing God has created, the most wonderful thing God has made, is humanity.

Even those who see humanity simply in naturalist terms must still affirm that this is the most developed and sophisticated form of life that we know. Even *Star Trek*'s Spock, the half-Vulcan/half-human of the *Starship Enterprise*, for all his knowledge, was only half-human, and Data, with his computerized mind, desperately desired to be human and is regarded as inferior to his human co-workers.

If God be God, surely God must then be not just power and intelligence, but what we call "person," and this is not demeaning or diminishing our sense of God. It is not to claim that God is just like us. As we said in reference to the meaning of faith, when we speak of God as "Person," we mean that God is *the Person*. We are only dim reflections of personhood. God may be more than what we understand as person, but God must be at least what we understand ourselves to be.

If God, who is at least what we understand as person, is to become known to us in the fullest possible way that we can understand, it will be not just as power in nature or as the intelligent order of the universe. It must be as the greatest thing God has created. It must be as a person. If God is going to be known to us in the fullest way, it will be as a human being, as one of us! Christian faith claims God did this in Jesus Christ.

When we speak, then, of Incarnation, we mean that there is revealed in Jesus the very Person, the very "Character" of God. In the humanity of the One we call Christ is revealed the very essence of divinity, in the fullest way possible to our understanding.

Since when has the Pacific Ocean been poured into a pint cup, that the God of this vast universe should be fully comprehended in human words? Nevertheless, even a cupful of the Pacific Ocean reveals its quality.[172]

The Inevitability of the Cross

I have claimed that God must be at least as great as anything God has created, and that humanity, personhood, is the highest development of God's creation (at least in terms of our present knowledge). What then is the highest expression of our humanity, our personhood?

I suggested in Chapter 5 that God's justice transcends our common conceptions of justice. It operates on a higher, or deeper, level. The love of God both fulfills our concept of justice and renders it irrelevant. "God's ways are not our ways, nor are God's thoughts our thoughts" (Isaiah 55:8). Jesus used the seeming amorality of nature, the sun that shines upon the evil and the good and the rain that falls on the just and the unjust, to point to the transcendent justice and mercy of God.

We noted that we have deep within us the demand for morality and justice—the expectation of "fair play" on the sports field and even in the business world. We dream of and strive for a just society and a just world order. This demand for common justice transcends the "law of the jungle." By it, some semblance of human law and order is maintained. We are able to contain our instinct for self-preservation at the expense of others by the ability to ensure our own existence by allowing others their existence as well. By our capacity for moral justice, not only our own life and goods, but our institutions and social order are sustained.

Yet Jesus points His disciples to "a righteousness that exceeds that of the scribes and Pharisees," that system of justice which is based upon "an eye for an eye and a tooth for a tooth." I suggested that there is a human quality and capacity that transcends our capacity for "proximate justice" (a term used by Reinhold Niebuhr to indicate that human justice is never perfect or absolute but

---

[172] Harry Emerson Fosdick, *Dear Mr. Brown: Letters To A Person Perplexed About Religion*, Harper and Row, Publishers, New York and Evanston, 1961, p. 37. (Fosdick is speaking of the use of words to speak of God.)

always proximate). That quality is the kind of self-giving and sacrificial love we see in Jesus.

We see this same love in the quality of family life, the care of a mother for her child, a child for elderly parents, even brothers and sisters, reaching beyond the demands of moral justice. We see it sometimes in marvellous ways reaching beyond the confines of family life and transcending the ordinary limits of the expectations of justice. "No one has greater love than this, to lay down one's life for one's friends" (John 13:13).

I'm pointing to our capacity to love, to give to and care for another beyond all reasonable expectation. This is what the New Testament calls *agape*. This capacity of self-giving, self-sacrificing love is the highest expression of our human personhood. Then, if we can say that this love is the highest expression of what we can become, we must say that God must be at least love! And God must surely express this quality absolutely!

Here is the essence of divinity, that which we must know if we are to know the Person of God. To know the love of God is the basis of our faith, the basis of our trust in God, and hence the basis of our security (salvation).

THE TEACHING OF JESUS

Consider how this higher morality, this caring and forgiving love that we call "grace," this "morality beyond morality," is so prominent in all that Jesus taught.

> You have heard it was said, "An eye for an eye and a tooth for a tooth." But I say to you, do not resist one who is evil. If anyone strikes you on the right cheek, turn the other also. And if anyone would sue you and take you coat, let him have your overcoat as well. And if anyone forces you to go one mile, go two. Give to anyone who begs from you, and do not refuse anyone who would borrow from you.

> You have heard that it was said, "You shall love your neighbour and hate your enemy." But I say to you, love your enemies and pray for those who persecute you, so that you may be children of your Father in heaven, who makes His sun to shine on the evil and on the good, and send rain on the just and the unjust (Matthew 5:38-45).

Jesus here points us to a higher realm of morality, beyond the realm of our calculated justice and limited righteousness, to that transcendent goodness of God which is like the sun, shining on the evil and on the good and like the rain falling on the just and on the unjust. He pointed His followers not to justice, but to love, love even of our enemies, those who would destroy us.

Our tendency would be to extend our charity only to the deserving, to give only to those whom we feel are worthy of our gift. That's only good stewardship.

Yet Jesus points out how different God is, for He loves those who are not deserving of His love, and has mercy on those who do not merit His mercy. Jesus takes what seems to be a complete lack of morality and justice in the realm of nature and uses this seeming amorality to point to the transcendent goodness of God, who "makes the sun to shine upon the evil and the good, and sends rain upon the just and the unjust." That same seemingly indifferent nature, which drives so many to futility and despair, is used by Christ to show the impartial goodness, the transcendent mercy, of God.

After all, to give only to the deserving is not charity. Charity is only charity when it is extended to the undeserving and the unworthy. Grace, which is the charity, the *caritas*, of God, is never fully merited or deserved.

> You often say, "I would give, but only to the deserving." The trees in your orchard say not so, nor the flocks in your pasture. They give that they may live, for to withhold is to perish. Surely he who is worthy to receive his days and his nights is worthy of all else from you. And he who has deserved to drink from the ocean of life deserves to fill his cup from your little stream.[173]

THE LAW OF GOD

The scripture quoted above (Matthew 5:38-45) is taken from those chapters of the Gospel of Matthew that we call "the Sermon on the Mount." Here, in part, Jesus presents us with an exposition of "the Law," the Ten Commandments.

---

[173] Kahlil Gibran, "On Giving," *The Prophet*, Alfred A. Knopf, New York, 1960, p. 21.

It's as though He is saying to the righteous people of the time, those who claimed that they have kept the Law, "You claim to do the will of God? Listen, here is the will of God." And He went on to interpret the Ten Commandments in such a way that no one can claim to have "fulfilled the Law."

> *You have heard it said, "You shall not kill!" But I say to you that whoever is angry with another harbours murder in her heart ...*
>
> *You have heard it said, "You shall not commit adultery!" But I say to you that whoever looks at a woman with lust has committed adultery with her already in his heart.*
>
> *If your right hand causes you to offend, cut it off and throw it away, for it is better for one of your members to perish than your whole body be cast into hell* (Matthew 5:21f, 27f.)

And in a desperate attempt to keep this saying, Origen, one of the fathers of the early church, castrated himself.[174]

By Jesus' teaching, who can say that he or she has never harboured anger? What man can say that he has never lusted after a woman? Anyone who says, "I never go to church, but I live by the Ten Commandments and the Sermon on the Mount," has obviously not read the Sermon on the Mount. Of course, those who go to church have not fully kept these instructions of Jesus either.

"Turn the other cheek," "If you have two coats, give to the one who doesn't have a coat," "Give to anyone who begs of you, and do not refuse anyone who would borrow from you." How impractical these precepts are. And yet, how right they seem.

If this is the will of God, who among us can claim to be righteous? We must all be dependent upon the charity, the *caritas*, the grace and mercy of God.

Again, Jesus taught, in the prayer he gave his disciples, "Forgive us our sins, as we forgive those who sin against us." And He continued immediately, as though it was the most important part of the prayer,

---

[174] Note Robert Payne, *The Holy Fire: The Story Of The Fathers Of The Eastern Church*, Harper & Brothers, New York, 1957, pp. 43, 45-46.

For if you forgive others their sins, your heavenly Father will also forgive you. But if you don't forgive others, neither will your heavenly Father forgive your sins (Matthew 6:14-15).

If we ask for justice, the same justice we demand will be used to judge us. If we seek mercy for ourselves, we must ourselves be merciful!

JESUS AS THE EMBODIMENT OF FORGIVING LOVE

Consider how Jesus embodied in Himself this forgiving, sacrificial love. In its name, He continually overstepped the laws of propriety of the time. In the name of that same love, He broke even the Law of the Sabbath, regarded as one of the most sacred of the Laws of God. He was called "the friend of tax collectors and sinners," those regarded as unworthy of either the love of God or of any social acceptance. He cared for the lame and the blind, for the leper and the unclean. He cared for the poor, the powerless, and the outcast.

From the early days of His ministry, He ran headlong into conflict with the authorities of the time. Not that He plotted violence and revolution, but it seems, almost from the first, that the principalities and powers of the time sensed that He was a threat to their traditions, their authority, to the very structure and order of their society.

And when they finally arrested Him, tried Him, and condemned Him to death, the basis of their condemnation was not that He was a thief or a murderer, but a blasphemer and traitor, that He claimed to be king, Messiah, the Christ. And on Golgotha (Calvary), they hanged Him upon a cross, driving nails through His hands and feet. And there, in what George Grant once called the supreme accomplishment of human history, He cried, "Father forgive them, for they know not what they do" (Luke 23:34).

He is the fulfillment of what He taught. He is the embodiment of the One who loves even the enemy. "Herein is love, not that we loved God, but that God loved us, and sent His Son to die for our sins" (I John 4:10).

Now we are faced with a paradox, and a powerful one at that. The self finds its fulfillment in the love through which the self gives and sacrifices itself. The justice by which the self seeks the continuation and perpetuation of its existence, paradoxically, never provides the self with the fulfillment it desires. The self finds its greatest fulfillment and happiness in giving itself in this forgiving and sacrificial love. But the self cannot give itself completely.

Let me put that another way. We find our human fulfilment, our greatest happiness, in this self-giving and sacrificial love which we know in Jesus. But we can only maintain our own existence, it seems, by human systems of law and justice, though these can never provide us with the fulfilment of our humanity and the happiness which we desire. For we find our fulfilment and happiness in this sacrificial love. But we cannot give ourselves completely and continually without any thought of ourselves, without feelings and thoughts of self-concern.

I speak from my own experience. At one point in my life, I tried so very hard to give myself to God, to give myself completely. I tried, I really tried, to love God with all my heart and soul and strength and mind, as the commandment requires. Surrender, they said. I tried hard to surrender. Let go and let God, they said. I tried so hard to let go. I prayed, I fasted, I read the Bible. I was indeed very religious. Finally, on a student mission field in the bush country of Saskatchewan, trying to living on salami and cheese, bread and milk, trying to bring in the Kingdom of God single-handed, I was thrown on my back, in hospital with pneumonia. I had to give up, to say, "Lord God, I can't. It must be up to You."

Gradually, I came to realize that this was also the experience of others. Saul the Pharisee, after trying to keep the Law, became Paul the Apostle and preached the wonderful freedom he found in Jesus Christ. He found that he couldn't know "righteousness," a right relationship with God, through his own efforts. He was dependent on the grace of God.

Augustine of Hippo, recognizing the limits of his own will, found another "mode of being which was altogether beyond the will."[175]

Or look to Martin the monk, who called on von Staupitz, vicar in his Augustine monastery, to hear his confession. "He confessed frequently, often daily, for as long as six hours on a single occasion. Every sin, in order to be absolved, had to be confessed,"

---

[175] Robert Payne, *The Fathers of the Western Church*, Dorset Press, New York, 1951, p. 148.

until finally Staupitz told him, "Come in with something to forgive—parricide, blasphemy, adultery—instead of all these peccadilloes."[176]

When the self, unable or unwilling to do what seems to be required of it, and seeking to maintain its existence through its capacity for moral justice, is confronted with this forgiving and sacrificial Love, the very grace of God in Jesus whom we call Christ, it finds its very existence threatened. We must, it would seem, seek to destroy that which would seem to destroy us!

Even more so, when those expressions of our corporate self, our human institutions and social orders, our business corporations and nation states and, yes, also our institutional churches, are confronted by the demands of this same love, demanding that they take no interest in their own welfare or maintenance, they too will resist, and even resort to violence. To seek to respond to such demand would seem tantamount to institutional suicide.

When the expression of that love is absolute, and the demand that it makes is also absolute, surely we can understand that our human systems could not tolerate, but must destroy, that which would seem to bring about its very destruction. That love, embodied in Jesus, had to be destroyed.

Such a forgiving and sacrificial Love, being true to itself, must accept its own destruction at the hands of a human capacity for moral justice. Remember again, it was not the forces of human evil that crucified Jesus. It was the systems of human justice and religion, Roman justice and Jewish religion. Their motives and intents were not necessarily evil, at least not in their own eyes. They considered Jesus' crucifixion necessary, or at least expedient. Caiaphas is quoted as saying, "It is expedient for you that one man should die for the people, and that the whole nation should not perish" (John 11:50).

On Calvary, there were three crosses. Two bore criminals, those who did not meet the standards of society, the common, decent laws of morality and retributive justice by which civilization has survived over the years, and so they had to die. The third

---

[176] Roland Bainton, *Here I Stand: A Live of Martin Luther*, Now American Library, Abingdom Press, Nashville, 1950, p. 41.

cross bore the body of the One who so transcended the ordinary goodness, morality, and justice of human society, and therefore seemed to threaten the stability of human morality and justice, that he, too, had to die. He taught that love, which we find so difficult to maintain even within our own families, was to be the law of all life, extending beyond family and friends, beyond countrymen and others of good will, even to our enemies and those who would destroy us. Such a threat to the social order had to be destroyed.

He was not crucified by bad or wicked people, but by good, respectable people, the upholders of justice and order of the time, righteous and religious people, people like us. In his love, our pretensions to moral and legal righteousness, our graceless goodness, are still condemned. But that same sacrificial and forgiving love is also our hope, the pattern of the life God has purposed for us, the possibility of the fulfillment of our humanity, our wholeness, and our salvation.

I have tried to show, beginning with the most elementary questions about ourselves and the world around us, an essential reasonableness in Christian faith and in the cross of Christ. The most complete way that God could possibly be revealed to us would have to be through the greatest that God has created (and which we can understand)—that is, as a Person, a human being! And so we believe that to speak of Jesus Christ as "God Incarnate" makes a certain sense.

God would then only be revealed through the highest qualities that human personality could express—forgiving and sacrificial Love, the fulfillment and destruction of the human demand for justice.

The cross was the inevitable result of such a transcendent Love, in its complete and ultimate expression, being confronted by our human capacity for moral justice.

> *God is Love, and God's Love is shown to us in this, that He sent His only Son into the world to bring us life. This Love of which I speak is not our love for God, but the Love God showed to us in sending His Son to die for our sins* (I John 4:9-10).

The fulfillment, the epitome of humanity, is the essence of divinity.

It Stands to Reason

It was a quiet Sunday night gathering in our living room. Some of our friends and parishioners drew together around a fire to meet and chat with one of the leading religious figures of our time. After he had made a few preliminary remarks, he said he would like to hear our questions and discuss them.

There were a few questions and some discussion, and then one of those short silences. One of the men, a businessman with a reputation for being aggressive, cut through the silence and said, "You know, sometimes I wonder what it's really all about. I know we're taught certain beliefs and doctrines, and we're told to believe them. But behind it all, what is there, really? I mean, *who is God?*"

There was earnestness in the way the question was asked. There was silence. For the next five minutes or so, I found myself quite oblivious to what was going on in the room, to the answer given by the visiting "expert." I was thinking about the question. How would I answer it, honestly? What did I believe about God, really?

I have claimed that we do really need God. I have claimed that this God we need is not the god we want. The god or gods we want are ones that will serve us, that will give us what we desire. The God we need is the One the Bible calls "the Lord," who calls us to a life of forgiving and sacrificial love.

If we examine all the evidence our experience has brought us, we may well agree that the balance would indicate a God of some kind, but the evidence is so confusing and ambiguous that we conclude that if there is some sort of god, a Creator, we really can't know what the deity is like.

The power of our intellect, our human ability to reason, to categorize, order and relate, may take us a long way in understanding the mystery of God, but we will only know the Person of God in Jesus, the One we call the Christ. We will only know the heart of God in the cross, the symbol of God's unlimited sacrificial love, that love which transcends human justice, which the New Testament calls by the Greek word, *agape*.

The two central and essential Christian doctrines that proclaim or explain this are the Incarnation and the cross. The God of Christian faith is known through Jesus' humanity, His life and death.

To the many, many people who say, "I believe in the teaching of Jesus, but I don't believe Jesus was the Son of God," to whom the Incarnation seems an impossibility, a paradox, a contradiction of reason, I offer an essential reasonableness to the belief that "God was in Christ" (II Corinthians 5:19). In the phrase adopted by traditional Christian orthodoxy, Jesus was both "fully human and fully divine." I believe that it is reasonable to assert that the seemingly most unreasonable and foolish of all religious symbols, the cross, also stands up to reason. In fact, I believe and affirm that the crucifixion of Jesus was inevitable.

Again, I don't mean to suggest that faith is simply a matter of reason. If God were subject to reason, then of course, reason would be God! If you could prove the existence of God by logic, then God's existence would be subject to that proof. God would no longer be God. God's very existence would be dependent upon something outside of God.

But that's not to suggest that faith must be unreasonable. There may be a kind of primitive Gnosticism, a more direct and personal way of knowing and walking with Jesus our risen Lord, which never questions the reality. It doesn't need to, because it knows Him, personally. It may, in fact, be that there are those pragmatic souls who sense in Jesus' teaching and ministry the active, living Spirit of God and whose lives bear witness to that commitment. But for those of the modern, doubting, questioning mind, I speak out of my own faith and reason. I hope, I pray, that I have shown that faith, the goodness of God, life after life, and even the Incarnation itself are all quite reasonable, and why even the cross not only makes sense, but also was really unavoidable.

CHAPTER 8

"ONCE UPON A TIME..."

*"For faith comes by hearing,
and hearing by the Word of God."*
(Romans 10:17)

A Picture of Christian Faith and Life

Children do like stories. They come to Mother or Father, or a grandparent, or a babysitter, or friend of the family, with their favourite storybook in hand, and say, "Read me a story, Daddy" (or whoever is the chosen story-reader of the moment). And though you have perhaps read the story a hundred times already, you settle down with your little bundle of love beside you, open the book, and begin to read,

"Once upon a time..."

Picture it. It's one of the loveliest of pictures. There is the one telling the story. There is the child, listening with eager anticipation and impatience as the story unfolds. And there is the unseen but dynamic interaction between the story and the child, the listening, the expectation, the waiting.

Here is a picture of Christian faith and life. There is the Story, the Gospel, the "Good News," the "Word of God." There is the one who hears, the seeker, the believer—perhaps you, or me. And there is the impatient waiting as the story unfolds, the listening, which for the Christian is akin to what the New Testament calls faith.

For "faith comes by hearing, and hearing by the Word of God" (Romans 10: 17 AV).

The Story—the Word of God

Preaching, at its best, is simply telling a story, the old, old story of God's love in Jesus Christ, how He came to seek and to save that which was lost. Though we preachers may often harangue the poor people in the pews about money and morals and going to church more regularly, surely we are being most true to our calling when what we say helps each waiting soul to believe in the goodness and the grace of God, so that faith and trust in God are instilled in the hearts of all who hear.

Preaching is telling the Story, and the greatest and best preachers have been the storytellers.

When you stop to think of it, the Bible itself (which we call "the Word of God") is basically a storybook. Not a book of rules for religious living or a manual on ecclesiastical order. Not a science book to give us a scientific account of creation. Not a history book to tell us how the human race was begun. The Bible may contain samples of all of these, but the Bible is mostly a storybook, the book of "the mighty acts of God," as scholars sometimes call it.

When all the texts have been interpreted and every last commentary has been written and the last great scholar has retired, the stories will still be there in all their simplicity for the child-like and the pure-in-heart to read and enjoy.

In the beginning, when God created the heavens and the earth, the earth was a formless void and darkness covered the face of the deep. And the Spirit of God moved over the face of the waters, and God said, "Let there be light." And there was light (Genesis 1:1f.)

And there were in that same country, shepherds, abiding in the field, keeping watch o'er their flocks by night. And lo, the angel of the Lord appeared to them and the glory of the Lord shone round about them, and they were sore afraid (Luke 2:8f.)

On the first day of the week, at early dawn, they came to the tomb bearing spices which they had prepared. They found the stone rolled away from the tomb, but when they went in, they did not find the body. Two men in dazzling clothes stood beside them and said, "Why do you look for the living among the dead. He is not here. He is risen!" (Luke 24:1f.)

The Gospel itself is a story, not a philosophical system or a moral code. It's the "Good News." As one preacher put it,

> Christianity, at bottom, is a story. When one has pushed the philosophy of religion and systematic theology and Biblical exegesis as far as they will go, when one has probed the best minds one can find as deeply as one can probe, then, as Frederick Buechner put it, "he is forced to take off his spectacles and push his books off to one side, and say, 'Once upon a time...!'"[177]

Now this is what is meant by "the Word of God"—the telling of the Story, God's Spell, the Gospel, the Good News of God's grace in Jesus Christ our Lord.

The Child—Hearing

We are the ones to whom the story is being told. We are "the child," and like little children, our part is to listen. We are to "hear." Again and again, the Bible asks us to do just this, before anything else: "Hear the Word of the Lord."

> *Hearken diligently unto me....*
> *Incline your ear....*
> *Hear, and your soul shall live.*
> (Isaiah 55:2-3, RSV)

For "faith comes by hearing."

The Story began with the creation, continued with promises and detours, triumphs and tragedies, culminating in the reality we call Jesus Christ. There's a sense in which the Gospel is about the end of the Story, how it all comes out—about the outcome of human history, about the outcome of each human life. It's the promise that someday the Prince will come and wake Sleeping Beauty with a kiss.

---

[177] Edmund Steimle's sermon "Wait!" in *Union Seminary Quarterly Review*, published by Union Theological Seminary,, New York City, Vol. XXII, No. 2, January, 1967, pp. 139-140.

But we're still in the middle of the story, each one of us, worried about what will happen next, like the child anxious to see how it all will turn out in the end. "We are in the middle of the play," says Amos Wilder. "The rounding off is ... in some sense still to come." [178]

We sit, quiet as little children listening to a story, considering no doubt the story of our own lives, what has happened to us of good or evil, wondering what will happen next and perhaps wondering how it will all come out in the end. We sit thinking of our children, our finances, our careers, our exams coming up, our triumphs and our failures, our joys and our sorrows. For the excitement of the story is always in what's about to happen, and how it will all turn out.

We ourselves are caught up in the story, for we are a part of the story, sharing the fears and thrills as it unfolds. We are afraid of what may happen, eager for the time when the Prince will come, the enemy be destroyed, and peace and joy be restored to the kingdom, and "all live happily ever after."

The Listening—Faith

But the end is not yet here, and for now we must wait! And, like little children, we don't like to wait.

Waiting is so desperately hard, and takes such a long, long time to learn. The young child desperately wants Sleeping Beauty to wake from her terrible sleep, but the story says that she must sleep until the Prince comes to wake her.

It seems that God is continually saying to us, "Just be patient. Wait a while, and everything will work out as it's supposed to." But we, like restless children, are so impatient.

Have you ever noticed in the Bible this word "wait?" It's there so often, and so often at the centre of what's happening.

Wait on the Lord, be of good courage, and God shall strengthen your heart. Wait, I say, on the Lord (Psalm 27:14).

---

[178] Amos Niven Wilder, *The Language Of The Gospel: Early Christian Rhetoric*, Harper and Row, New York, 1964, p. 67

They that wait upon the Lord shall renew their strength. They shall put forth wings as eagles. They shall run and not be weary. They shall walk, and not faint (Isaiah 40:31).

Blessed are they that wait upon the Lord, for they shall inherit the earth (Psalm 37:9).

The Old Testament is full of waiting—prophets forecasting and the people waiting for the action of God, waiting for the coming of the "Prince," God's Messiah.

And yet in the church, we who believe that "Messiah is come," we too continue to wait, for the people of God live in a manner of having and yet not having. We "live by faith."[179]

What we call "faith" is very nearly what the Old Testament calls "waiting on the Lord." Richard Luecke says,

> It is in waiting for the Lord that the very reality of faith is unfolded, because faith implies a certain not having and not knowing.... It is in waiting that God is God and not an idol, that faith is faith and not superstition.[180]

There are two dimensions to the meaning of the word "wait" in the Bible. One is what the word is more apt to mean to some of us— the tedium and boredom of waiting for the repairs to be completed so that our flight can take off, waiting in line to register, to see the doctor, or to hear the report of the biopsy.

Sometimes this kind of waiting can be much more difficult. There can be so much at stake. Have you ever in your life had one of those periods when everything seemed to go wrong, one disaster after another, and every move you made seemed to be the wrong one? You fight to keep going, just to hang on, in the belief that sooner or later things just have to change!

There are those among us who are older and know what this is, have learned it the only way it can be learned: the hard way. I am told by a friend of Ukrainian ancestry that the Ukrainians, with their long history of deprivation and suffering, have a word for

---

[179] In Chapter 4 we discussed the meaning of faith, realizing faith not as spiritual willpower nor as assent to dogma but as trust in the grace and goodness of God.

[180] Richard Lueke, *New Meanings For New Beings*, Harper and Row, New York, 1964, pp. 50-51

it—*terpiachuk*, "endurance factors," that which enables one to hang on when everything seems lost. Here is faith that is tested, and in trial is made strong.

This kind of waiting makes us come to terms with God's patience, that utterly maddening patience of His, as if God had all eternity to work things out, when your time and mine is so short.[181]

This is closer to what waiting in the Bible is like—the dogged, hanging-on-for-dear-life faithfulness that stands against disappointment and disillusionment as the hopes of the people are smashed again and again.

Yet there are always those who, with oil in their lamps (note Matthew 25:1-12), wait for the Lord. The Bible calls them "the meek," or "the poor in spirit"—those like young Mary, the peasant girl of Galilee, who didn't seem at all surprised when the angel appeared to her. This was at a time of special hopelessness in Israel's history, when Rome was the oppressor and for a very long time there had been no "Word from the Lord."

But there's another aspect to what the Bible means by waiting. There is a passive kind of waiting, a hanging-in-there kind of waiting. There is also an active aspect to waiting. There is, for instance, the picture in Psalm 130, the picture of the watchman sensing that the long night is almost past and the new day about to dawn, straining his eyes to the eastern sky to see the first light of new day.

> *I wait for the Lord ... and in God's Word do I hope. My soul waits for the Lord—more than they that watch for the morning. I say, more than they that watch for the morning* (Psalm30:5-6).

There's nothing patient about that, or about that verse in Romans 8 where Paul writes that "the whole world waits in eager anticipation for the revealing of the sons of God" (Romans 8:19). Phillips translates that as "the whole creation stands on tip-toe."[182]

Here is a kind of waiting more appreciated and understood by those of us who are younger, who haven't yet learned the patience of older years, and who want to take the story into their own hands by rushing straight to its ending, grabbing Sleeping Beauty and

---

[181] Steimle, op. cit., p. 44
[182] J. B. Phillips, *The New Testament in Modern English*, Geoffrey Bles, London, 1960.

shaking her awake, with violence if necessary, for the Prince is much too long in coming.

This is part of waiting too—the kind of importunate praying that keeps tugging at God's coat-tail saying, "Come on, get on with it, for Christ's sake!" It's the kind of impatient expectation that sends us out to meet Him, out into the wilderness of the world to "prepare the way of the Lord." By getting things all tidied up, by keeping the Sabbath law perfectly just once, by seeing that all the hungry are fed, by achieving peace and justice for all, by marching in demonstrations and holding high our banners, so we may hurry Him up and hasten the ending of the story.

You see, the word "wait" must mean both of these. Waiting without expectation and anticipation would no longer be waiting. Where there is no longer hope, we go home, or fall asleep. Without the patience, the dogged endurance, even when all hope seems gone, there, too, waiting stops, and in our youthful impatience we either try to force the issue or turn to something else in which the results are more immediately apparent.

The root of the biblical word "wait" is a verb meaning "to stretch." There's a tension in it that demands of us patience until the story has run its course, and at the same time keeps us awake, hoping, expecting, praying, and working. It's all right there at the very end of the Bible, almost the last words:

> The one who gives this testimony speaks: "Yes, I am coming soon!" Amen. Even so, come, Lord Jesus (Revelation 22:20).

And as Joseph Sittler says, Christian life is "drawn taut between the Amen and the Come."[183] For Christian life is lived between memory and hope.

It's all there. The Story is the Word of God! And we are the hearers, those who listen. Then let us listen, each one, listen to it ourselves, again and again—waiting on the Lord, anxiously, expectantly, with all the bubbling excitement of a little child, but also patiently, knowing that the story must run its course and that the end will come in all its glory, but only in God's good time.

---

[183] Joseph Sittler, *The Ecology Of Faith*, Muhlenberg Press, Philadelphia, 1961, p. 104

A Commissioning

We are called to be not just children hearing the story, but those who convey and seek to enact the message. We are not little children passively listening to a story about someone else. We are participants in the story; it's *our* story. We are, as the New Testament says, "co-workers with God," meaning that we do have at least some influence on the development of the plot, of the action (in the dramatic sense). We may be creatures of history, but we are also to some extent creators of history.

So we are not just to listen. We are also called to tell the Story so that, in the telling, others too may know their parts. We "tell the Story" by being faithful to what we believe to be good and right, even when there is no profit in it, even when the wise cynics with dog-like cunning are able to mass evidence against it. [184] We tell the Story by doing things with our lives that only a fool would do—a fool for Christ. We tell the Story by sharing our own faith and experience of the grace and goodness of God as it has touched our own lives.

We don't all need to be preachers. We can tell it by word, by song, by being faithful and showing grace in what we do and who we are.

One winter, I had a 75-year-old Baptist minister working with me. He had a bad heart, and when he climbed the stairs to the Church Office, you could hear him stop on the landing, gasping to catch his breath. But Percy Hayden would go into the room or home of someone who was sick, old, and lonely, even someone who we would say "had nothing to live for," and after a short visit and prayer leave that person with a feeling of happiness and peace.

Following his retirement, Percy made a habit of always memorizing the scripture lesson, and would stand at the pulpit and recite it, the words flowing from him graciously with a beatific smile on his face. Our congregation nicknamed him "Happy Hayden."

---

[184] The word "cynic" comes from the Greek word *kunos*, meaning dog.

His wife once told me that when he got up in the morning, he would stand at the window in his nightshirt, spread his arms, and say, "Thank you, Lord, for another wonderful day!"

He was a man who, through every quality of his life, told and lived the Story.

There was another story my mother used to tell, which I still cherish. As a young woman, she worked as a private duty nurse in a large city. Her patient was a woman who was suffering a great deal and was nearing the end of her life.

Also in this city was another woman, a singer who, before marrying and settling there, had been famous in her time as a concert artist. Through the long, painful hours of the evening and into the night, the sick woman mentioned several times how much it would mean to hear her sing.

Finally, late at night and realizing that her patient would probably not live to see the morning, my mother went to the phone and was bold enough to ask the great lady if she would come. And though the hour was late, the distance great and the trip difficult, she replied, "Yes, I'll come at once."

My mother used to say, "I'll always remember that night when she stood by the bedside of a dying woman and sang softly,

> Jesus loves me, loves me still,
> Though I'm very weak and ill.
> From his shining throne on high,
> Comes to watch me where I lie.[185]

We have a wonderful story to tell, and live. God is gracious. We know God's grace in the life and death and resurrection of our Lord and Saviour Jesus Christ. Into that grace we can trust ourselves, our hearts and lives, those we love, and all that is. That is faith.

Ours need not be a troubled faith. It is faith that stands up to reason. It is a realistic faith, an empowering faith. It is a faith that, through the cross of Jesus Christ, may even be a triumphant faith.

---

[185] "Jesus loves me," by Anna Bartlett Warner, *The Hymnary*, op. cit., No. 623.